THE NEW PROTECTIONISM

By

J. A. HOBSON

First published in 1916

British Library Cataloguing-in-Publication Data
A catalogue record for this book is available
from the British Library

The tendency of all strong Governments has always been to suppress liberty, partly in order to ease the processes of rule, partly from sheer disbelief in innovation.

J. A. HOBSON

CONTENTS

PREFACE

It is not my purpose in these chapters to traverse the whole field of controversy between Protectionists and Free Traders, cultivated so intensively during the years following the Chamberlain proposals of 1903-1905. During this war the fiscal problem has taken a new aspect. Protectionists have found in the associations and divisions among nations imposed by war, and the necessities or expediencies of war economics, a new fund of hope and opportunity for the achievement of their objects. During the war the enemy's trade is part of the enemy's war resources, and is rightly made an object of attack. In the general atmosphere of international antagonism it is not difficult to represent this same trade as inimical to our interests and a potential source of danger to our country even in time of peace. The revival and growth of German industry and commerce after the war will, it is urged, enable Germany to prepare for another war. We must therefore do all we can to prevent that revival and retard that growth. Moreover, German business men subordinate their private profit-seeking to political ends, dumping goods, invading markets, driving wedges of finance, in order that the " economic domination " thus obtained may be placed at the service of a powerful aggressive State. This State they see combining with and subjugating its neighbours, so as to form a powerful political and economic system of Central Europe, which will reach out its commercial and financial tentacles so as to drag in other neutral countries. This huge menace of a future German world-power, political and economic, and, when the time comes, military, is paraded before the heated and confused imagination of our people by our New Protectionists.

My object is to inspect and test, first, the substance of this economic menace, and, secondly, the validity of the measures by which it is proposed to meet it. The New Protectionism differs from the Old in seeking to superimpose the present war map of the world, with its divisions of belligerents, allies, and neutrals, upon the Protectionism of 1903-1905, which sought to combine protection for British industries with a closer business connection between the self-governing dominions and the mother-country. To extract a definite intelligible shape for this New Protectionism out of the general rhetoric in which it is embedded by most of its exponents is no easy task. Its principal organs in the Press—such as the *Morning Post*, the Northcliffe papers, and by recent conversion the *Spectator* — do not agree among themselves either as to scope, objects, or methods; and the Chambers of Commerce—more concerned with business and less with politics—formulate proposals woefully deficient in that element of " defence " which is of primary importance to political enthusiasts.

The single fact which ought to guide us in our interpretation of the New Protectionism is that the moving and moulding spirit is the evident desire of groups of business men to exploit the emotions of friendship and antagonism generated by the war and the immediate economic exigencies of the situation, in order a get a public policy which will yield them private profit. Multitudes of other men are moved by patriotic and other uncommercial motives to applaud and to promote a Protectionist policy, but all experience shows that they do little to determine the form that policy takes. The famous saying of Sir James Fitzjames Stephen, that "The world is made for hard practical men who know what they want and mean to get it," finds no more convincing corroboration than in the annals of Protection.

The perception of this central truth is doubtless obscured at present by the prominence given by war pressure to what is in its ultimate significance a sharp business enterprise. The Paris Conference, for example—a copy of the Report of which is here given as an appendix—focuses attention upon the Alliance as an economic system for the conduct of the war, and for defensive work afterwards. With the economic war policy itself I am not concerned to deal. But the measures proposed for common action during the period of reconstruction, and the permanent measures of mutual assistance and collaboration, raise issues of great moment for those who regard Free Trade as economically sound, and consider a policy aiming at a lasting severance between the present belligerent groups as a menace to the future peace of the world. Although the document nowhere explicitly commits this country to any tariff or other definitely Protectionist act, it lays down a line of policy which involves Protection. The very language of its preamble is replete with Protectionist assumptions. Our enemies are represented as preparing for " a contest on the economic plane." Their preparations " have the obvious object of establishing the domination of the latter (*i.e.*, the enemy) over the production and markets of the whole world, and of imposing on other countries an intolerable yoke. In face of so grave a peril, the representatives of the Allied Governments consider that it has become their duty—on grounds of necessary and legitimate defence—to adopt and realize from now onward all the measures requisite, on the one hand, to secure for themselves and for the whole of the markets of neutral countries full economic independence and respect for sound commercial practice; and, on the other hand, to facilitate the organization on a permanent basis of their economic alliance."

Now, in this book I examine the curious assumptions of this passage—the notion of trade as a "contest" in which one of the trading parties secures "domination" over the other, the notion that protective tariffs and other barriers are needed for " defence," and the notion that such " defence " can be successfully obtained by any of these methods. The assumption that German trade and finance are mainly and normally State instruments—departures from " sound commercial practice "—and that the Allies are called on not merely to defend themselves against this invasion and this domination, but also to secure the " independence " of the neutral markets, is a blend of naïveté and ignorance to which it is difficult to do full justice.

Though history lends little support to the conviction that war alliances are of so firm and durable a nature as to afford a reliable basis for far-sighted business arrangements, Free Trade has nothing but commendation for proposals for closer and more effective trade relations between allies, provided they are not intended, and do not in fact work out, as a policy of exclusion and hostility to other countries. Schemes for the improvement of transport, postal and other communications, for identical facilities in patent law, trade-marks, and copyright, as between the members of the allied countries, amount *pro tanto* to an extension of the area and liberty of human intercourse beyond the national barriers, and as such are in every way desirable.

But economic sanity regards with very different eyes the first heading of the " Permanent Measures "—viz., " Economic Independence of Enemy Countries," with its opening paragraphs. " The Allies decide to take the necessary steps without delay to render themselves independent of the enemy countries in so far as regards the raw materials and manufactured articles essential to the normal development of their economic activities. These measures should be directed to assuring the independence of the Allies, not only as regards their sources of supply, but also as regards their financial, commercial, and maritime organization."

Now, though neither here nor elsewhere in the Report is there any definite agreement to adopt a policy of Tariffs, Export Duties, Navigation Acts, Financial Boycott, or other specified weapons of Protectionism, the policy indicated is one which plainly involves, or indeed demands, the application of such measures. "Economic Independence" of the kind described, though it does not preclude all commerce with the Central Powers, clearly contemplates the exclusion from this country of most of the staple imports which have hitherto come in, such as sugar, steel and iron, machinery, glass and glassware, cotton and woollen yarns and goods. The organization of Allied commerce, finance, and maritime arrangements, for complete "independence" implies not merely prohibitory tariffs on large classes of goods, but legal measures for the exclusion of German capital from all employment in the Allied countries, and restrictive or prohibitive measures against German and Austrian shipping. Whether "independence" be interpreted as absolute exclusion, or as security against such economic intercourse as brings "dependence," it can only be compassed by methods of State preference or State boycott, which constitute a radical departure from the accepted economic policy of Great Britain. Whatever were the specific methods adopted to secure the object, it would have two economically and politically disastrous results. In the first place, by narrowing the area of our free external markets, it would diminish the total gains of British industry and commerce, and render more precarious the livelihood of a population and a trade dependent for existence upon large and assured access to varied sources of overseas supplies. Secondly, by breaking Europe into two nominally independent but really hostile and competing economic systems, it would foster conflicts in all parts of the world, maintain and feed the bitter memories of this war, stimulate the maintenance and growth of armaments, and render another war inevitable.

Moreover, the first aggressive step in this

"war after the war" would have been taken, not by the Central Powers, but by the Allies, and the false charge made by German publicists, that the main actuating motive of Great Britain in entering the war was jealousy of the growth of German trade and a desire to crush a trade rival, would receive a most specious corroboration. For though the Paris Report opens by the statement that "the Empires of Central Europe are to-day preparing, in concert with their allies, for a contest on the economic plane," there is no evidence that any single step has actually been taken towards this preparation. On the contrary, even the informal proposals that Austro-Hungary shall enter into some economic alliance with the German Empire, propounded many months ago, have met with such strenuous opposition both in Vienna and in Buda-Pesth that they appear to have been abandoned. The first effect of the Paris Conference, should it take shape in any practical measures of co-operation for an after-war trade policy, will be to give fresh vigour to the German advocates of an economic Middle Europe by enabling them to represent their scheme as a necessary defence against the economic warfare already announced by the Allies.

Another obvious vice of any binding economic arrangement made now by the Allies for operation after the war is that it impairs our freedom of action at the Peace Settlement for the all-important work of placing international relations upon a better basis of security. No League of Nations, such as President Wilson and Sir Edward Grey (to name but two of many important supporters of this plan) still contemplate as possible, could come into existence if, at the close of the military conflict, the two belligerent groups had already committed themselves to a permanent war of commerce.

These considerations give the gravest significance to the concluding paragraph of the Paris Report, in which " the representatives of the Allied Governments undertake to recommend their respective Governments to take without delay all the measures, whether temporary or permanent, requisite for giving full and complete effect to this policy forthwith." This indecent haste can only have one meaning so far as this country is concerned. It is designed to enable our Protectionists to reverse the permanent fiscal policy under cover of a war emergency, and by the aid of the hot passions and confused judgment which such a situation engenders. This interpretation is supported by the action taken by the Colonial Secretary, before the ink of this Report was dry, in directing the Colonies to impose forthwith, and for five years after the war, an export duty of £2 a ton upon all palm-kernels exported to foreign countries. Primarily directed to destroy the German manufactures of palm-oil, a basis of several important products, such as soap, margarine, and oil-cake, this return to our early colonial policy of preference for the home market will create alarm in all neutral foreign countries, and will, by enhancing the uncertainty of future trade, make a speedy return to normal industry after the war more difficult for every nation, belligerent or neutral.

The greater part of my argument concerns itself with a discussion of the economic results which would flow from the attempt to apply in practice the proposals of the New Protectionism. But in a concluding chapter I sketch the outlines of a constructive policy of " The Open Door," a rational alternative to the destructive policy of the New Protectionists, and designed to promote co-operation instead of conflict between the Governments of the commercial nations and the business groups who chiefly mould their foreign policy.

A portion of the argument was published recently in a series of articles in the *Manchester Guardian*, to the proprietors of which I am indebted for permission to make this further use of them.

J. A. HOBSON.

HAMPSTEAD,
   June 24, 1916.

THE NEW PROTECTIONISM

CHAPTER I

THE REVIVAL OF PROTECTIONISM

THE policy of Free Trade is based upon a reasoned belief that all commerce is an exchange between the goods or services of one person and those of another, this exchange being usually effected by two monetary transactions—an act of sale and an act of purchase. Both parties in such commerce are gainers from it, and their gains tend to be equal. The material advantage of this process is unaffected by the consideration that the two parties may be members of different political communities. The wider the area, the freer and more secure the nature of this intercourse, the greater is the net gain, both to those parties directly engaging in each act of commerce and to those who indirectly profit by doing business with parties thus enriched. The validity of this economy of co-operation by division of labour is as obvious in practice as in logic. Almost everyone admits it on a smaller scale, within the village, the province, the nation. It is only disputed when it is sought to apply it to the wider co-operation of men and businesses in the world at large.

There are one or two errors, common to all Protectionist proposals, fundamental in their character, which need to be exposed in the outset of every discussion of the subject.

The first is the presentation of nations as trading firms. Great Britain is treated as if she did business, in her corporate capacity, with Germany or the United States. The several commercial countries are also regarded as competing with one another for trade with other countries. Neither of these views is correct. Great Britain does not

trade with Germany; individual Britons
trade with individual Germans, buying from
them and selling to them, just as they do in
the case of fellow-Britons, each party seeking and finding his private gain from each
transaction. It is, of course, possible to
add together all these separate acts of sale
and purchase which take place between
members of the different nations, and put
them under the collective title British trade,
German trade, American trade. Our Board
of Trade returns do this, thus unintention-
ally conveying the suggestion that there is
something different in the economic nature
and value of overseas trade and purely
domestic trade.

If this suggestion that Great Britain as a
nation trades with Germany and the United
States is a mischievous falsehood, still more
mischievous is the suggestion that they are
hostile competitors for trade with other
countries. For this is a double-barrelled
falsehood. The first falsehood is the perversion of the actual fact that the competi-

tion for business, either abroad or at home, is usually far keener and more continuous between different British firms or different German and American firms among themselves than it is between a British firm and a German or an American firm. The second falsehood is the misrepresentation of such commercial competition as a struggle between two nations for a limited amount of profitable foreign market, which the one gains and the other loses. There is no such absolute limit to the quantity of foreign market. The notion that the expansion of foreign markets obtained within the last two decades by German or American traders is a corresponding loss of markets to British traders is sheer nonsense. To a large extent those markets were " created " by the special economic and commercial activities of the German or American trader. For the rest, an enlargement of our foreign markets which, in default of German or American competition, might have taken place, would have involved a diminution of our home markets.   There is no evidence that the advance of German or American foreign trade has caused productive power in this country to remain idle to any larger extent than when we were " the workshop of the world."

Sane consideration of the nature of commerce compels us to deny that the increased commerce of Germans or Americans has reduced the aggregate market for British goods.

This treatment of nations as trading units is the first item of the series of separatist fallacies upon which Protectionism old and new relies.

The second is the separation of the interests of the seller from those of the buyer, and the false assertion that the interests of the former are, or ought to be, superior.

The reason why Protectionism appeals to the producer and ignores the consumer is evident.   Every man contains within the limits of his own person the whole economy of world co-operation and exchange *in petto*. As producer he makes a large surplus of some one particular sort of goods, and exchanges this surplus against an infinite number of bits of surpluses of various kinds made by other specialized producers in all parts of the world. As producer he is one ; as consumer he is many. Now, as the productive side of his life absorbs the greater part of his conscious organized energy and attention, he comes to think it more important, and to regard it as severed in its nature from the consuming side. He looks more closely to the amount of money he receives, as profit or wages, than to the prices of the goods upon which he expends that money. This habitual separation of his producing from his consuming self, and the superior conscious stress upon the former, give the Protectionist his opportunity. He makes his separate appeal to the man as producer, tells him that selling is more important than buying, and that the money he receives is more important than what he can buy with it.

It is through consumption that the co-operative nature and value of commerce is realized. Production divides, consumption unites. Hence the appeal of the Protectionist to the nation as a body of producers.

For, when the Protectionist has once succeeded in getting the gain of the producer accepted as the sole test of sound economy, he is enabled to pursue his separatist tactics farther. He can appeal to a nation, not as a corporate union of producers, but as a number of separate producing groups. He can take each particular trade, or each locality, and invite it to consider whether a tariff upon the importation of the articles which this trade or this locality produces would not be beneficial to these producers, whether they be capitalists or workers. This so-called " practical " test of an appeal to local business interests appears at first sight incontrovertible. If Bradford could get high import duties upon woollen goods entering this country, it would have a monopoly of the home market, without losing any foreign market it was able to supply.

Similarly with Sheffield cutlery, with North-
ampton boots, or with any other local or
national industry.   It is easy to show how a
tariff can do good to each of them, taken
separately.   " But," argues the Protectionist,
" a policy which can be shown to be good for
each must surely be good for all."   This, of
course, is the central fallacy.   If the Bradford weaver gets Protection and nobody else,
he stands to gain.   But if all the other British
trades,   local   and   national,   engaged   in
making articles he needs in his trade—*e.g.*,
wool, coal, machinery, dyes, etc.—or articles
of food, clothing, furniture, etc., on which he
spends his wages, also get Protection, each
duty to protect those other trades filches
from him a bit of the gain he stood to make
if the Bradford woollen trade were alone
protected.   A general tariff protecting all
British trades equally would thus be found
to make so many deductions from the value
of the special Protection enjoyed by the
woollen trade, as to convert it from a gain
into a loss.   The higher prices of woollens

which his Protection enabled him to get would be outweighed by the added higher prices of the various articles required for use in his trade and for his private consumption. This appeal to the separate interests of each trade is sometimes known as " the distributive fallacy." It consists in arguing that what is true of each must be true of all. It is well illustrated in the hortatory method in vogue in American schools, where upon the Fourth of July the boys assembled are reminded that every one present is capable of becoming President of the United States, though it is evidently impossible that more than about ten in the whole country can attain the position.

The whole economics of Protection is thus seen to be rooted in the soil of separatism, disruption, and antagonism. Its policy is realized in a number of conflicting preferences and pulls, that of producer against consumer, trade against trade, locality against locality, capital against labour, land against both, and, lastly, nation against nation, falsely represented as economic corporations. At every point of cleavage damage is wrought upon the economy of human co-operation for the production, distribution, and exchange, of wealth.

But, it may well be asked, how has Protection been able to make so much way against the forces of reason and collective self-interest? How have separate group-interests succeeded in imposing a protective system in so many countries, and how are they able in this country to set on foot a powerful movement to overthrow the established fiscal system of Free Trade?

The history of the last half-century condenses into a few brief lessons the forces and conditions which have enabled certain particular business interests within a country to impose tariffs detrimental to the economic interests of the nation as a whole. The unequal organization of the several business interests within a nation for co-operative work in the field of politics is of prime importance. Modern capitalist development has everywhere given prominence to certain staple manufactures in textiles and metals, etc., which, by reason of their widespread utility and importance, assumed the chief rôle in foreign trade. It was natural that whatever aids Government could render to these wealthy, concentrated, enterprising trades, by way of safeguarding for them the possession of their domestic markets wherever seriously threatened, and of obtaining new foreign markets, should become objects of political endeavour among the members of these trades. To these staple textile and metal trades other important capitalist industries have sometimes attached themselves—*e.g.*, shipbuilding and shipping, chemicals, leather, etc.—bringing organized political pressure on their national Government to get tariff protection, bounties, railroad facilities, and various diplomatic and other political assistance in winning foreign markets. If the members of a few strong national trades can exercise a series of special pulls in the construction of a tariff, or the pursuance of an expensive or risky foreign policy adapted to their trade ends, the good of the nation as a whole, represented by a weak, diffused and ill-sustained opposition to their strong, concentrated and persistent policy, is likely to go to the wall. This has been the story of the rise and progress of Protectionism in all the countries where it has made way in recent times.

The strong organized trades have waited for, fostered, and utilized, special political emergencies in the history of their country. Wars and their financial aftermath have been the most-favoured emergencies. The financial embarrassment wars cause to Governments, coupled with the reluctance of statesmen to resort to the unpopular methods of a heavy increase of direct taxation, have commonly afforded the opportunity to the waiting Protectionists. The modern Protectionist policy of the United States was a direct legacy of the Civil War. Before that event the United States tariffs had been tending towards Free

Trade, the general level of the Act of 1857 being lower than that of any period since 1816. Afterwards, the Constitution not permitting of an income-tax, high tariffs were imposed, at first accompanied by excise duties ; soon the excise duties were withdrawn and the import duties remained.

The high Protection of France and Germany is attributable to similar causation, the pressure of war debts and fresh expenditure for armaments offering the Protectionist interests their opportunity. The return to high Protection by France in 1875, and in Germany a few years later, was not, indeed, wholly due to fiscal needs. Trade depression and unemployment, attributed to a dumping policy of British manufacturers, helped the movement towards a "national economy," the patriotic mask of naked business interests. In both countries the textile and metal trades were compelled to work in conjunction with the agricultural interest. This was due in Germany to the survival of the feudal power of the land-

owning class in the Government, especially
of Prussia ; in France to the widespread but
very strongly defined influence of the great
peasant electorate. This "balance of power"
between two economic forces of producers,
naturally opposed to one another, has brought
about curious fluctuations and compromises
in the protective policy of the two countries ;
but upon the whole it has worked, politically,
for the maintenance and elevation of tariffs.

But this seizure of special financial and
economic opportunities is not a full explana-
tion of the success of the Protectionist
movement. The whole tenor of political
history, with its excessive emphasis upon
the nation as the limit of sympathy and
corporate obligation for the citizen, and
upon the opposing interests and struggles
between nations, has furnished an education
and an emotional atmosphere favourable to
the acceptance of Protectionists' ideas of
national economy. In such an atmosphere,
even during times of peace, it has been easy
to impose on the common mind notions and

language which present trade in terms of international hostility. England, Germany, the United States, are rivals, fighting for markets, and taking markets that " belong " to " our nation," " stealing marches " upon us, and otherwise seeking to injure our trade. When within each State some group of business interests actually controls the foreign and fiscal policy, it does actually produce, by tariffs, shipping laws, commercial treaties, and a pushful colonial policy, a sufficient semblance of economic militarism to give plausible support to this fundamentally false conception of international trade. There does exist this real opposition between trading and financial groups and syndicates within the several nations, which by impudent misuse of language and of politics usurp the title of their respective States. So France, Great Britain, Germany, America, and Japan, may easily be represented as opposed to one another, in their national capacity, in a contest for trade and concessions in China, when the truth is that some tiny

little knot of pushful merchants or bankers
in each country, with or without the assistance of their Foreign Offce, are the actual
contestants.

If this is the normal modern situation, it
is easy to understand how the military policy
of States, the preparations for war, the conduct of war, and the sequelæ of war, play
into the hands of Protectionists.   In a
dangerous world, where a nation is exposed
to have its foreign trade cut off during war,
common prudence, it is held, must impel the
State to make arrangements enabling the
nation to be as self-sufficing as possible in
supplies of the requisites of civil existence
and military use.   A protective tariff is
advocated as a chief instrument for achieving
this "national economy."   So Protection is
urged, not as an instrument of national
wealth, but of national defence.   In continental Europe this consideration has been
paramount in modern times, when, with the
growth of population and improved facilities
of transport, the people of one country might

drift into a dangerous dependence on the people of adjoining countries for some necessary supplies. The fear lest war might cut them off from necessary foreign markets has been a weapon of immense value to the Protectionist interests in Germany, France, and other countries with potential enemies across their frontiers.

CHAPTER II

DEFENCE AND OPULENCE

In this country the revival of Protectionism is seen to be the immediate fruit of war and militarism. Groups of our traders, exposed to growing foreign competition in this country and in the markets of the world, had long striven to plant a protective tariff for British manufacturers upon the formal programme of the Conservative party. The landowners and farmers, injured by the long-continued fall of food prices, also brought what political pressure they could towards the protection of "the agricultural interests." But Free Trade had been too long a settled fiscal policy in this country to be easily disturbed; the difficulties of reconciling manu-facturing with agricultural Protection were too evident; "food taxes" were too unpopular an electoral cry; periods of trade depression and unemployment, the one real hope of our Protectionists, were not long enough or bad enough to serve the purpose.

The Boer War brought into play new emotional forces and a financial situation which seemed favourable for Tariff Reform. The war-borrowing left a larger indebtedness, and the new naval programme, taken in conjunction with the costs of long-due social reforms, like old-age pensions, brought a pressure on the public revenue which gave plausibility to any scheme for "broadening the basis of taxation." The rally of Imperialist sentiment in our self-governing dominions and their active support in the war gave a new, passionate emphasis to the notion of a self-sufficing Empire bound together by a system of mutually preferential tariffs. The bitter criticism of our policy upon the Continent, and the threats of concerted intervention in favour of the Boer Republics, left in our people a powerful anti-foreigner sentiment obviously useful as grist to the Protectionist mill.

Mr. Chamberlain and his Tariff Reformers were right in thinking the time favourable for their project. But it was not favourable enough. The financial solution was not grave enough ; the industrial depression did not respond to expectations ; the sentiment of Imperial unity was too vague; the advantages of good business relations with foreign countries were too obvious ; cheap food was too evidently advantageous to the working classes. Again, the Tariff Reformers did not get in their work in time. The glamour of militarist exploits had already faded, the debauch had left the country with a headache and the bill. The advocates of Protection in 1903 and the following years were unable to substitute sentiment and passion for reasoning and calculation. Hard · facts and the logic of the situation told too heavily against them. To persuade the nation that its trade was going to the dogs when common experience and official records proved the contrary, to persuade the mass of busy workers that tariffs were needed to cure unemployment, and that if they did pay more for their food they would get it back in other ways, proved too difficult a task.

The trouble in this earlier Protectionist campaign was that the trade interests operating it found the sentimental Imperialism, patriotism, and militarism deficient in volume and intensity to serve their purpose. They were forced into argument, and therefore beaten. Our New Protectionists, having a far greater and more various fund of sentiment and passion at their disposal, hope to avoid close economic controversy, or at any rate to reduce it to a wholly subordinate place in their campaign for tariffs. They have learnt this lesson. They will no longer find it necessary to prove that Protection raises wages, enlarges and secures employment, conserves and develops the natural resources of the country, directs foreign trade into more profitable channels, and performs the other economic miracles claimed for it by its advocates. These notions are doubtless still cherished by "true believers," but they are no longer needed for missionary work among "the heathen." Free Traders, or indifferents, are to be converted by quite a different appeal. That appeal is skilfully addressed to them in the admission of the great prophet of Free Trade, Adam Smith himself, that "Defence is much more important than Opulence." In other words, we are adjured to admit that mere quantity of wealth, mere volume of trade, mere cheapness, may be rightly sacrificed to the higher considerations of national or Imperial strength and security.

Now the truth of this general statement is indisputable. The emergencies of the war have furnished various illustrations of proper and necessary interferences with liberty of trades in the higher interest of national security. It has been deemed desirable to restrict or prohibit certain imports, so as to reduce the consumption of luxuries, liberate labour for useful services, economize shipping, and strengthen the foreign exchanges, to say nothing of the regulation and restriction of our export trade in order to conserve certain supplies for our own use or to prevent other supplies falling into enemy hands. Except as regards the detailed operation of the restrictions upon imports, Free Traders have fully acquiesced in these emergency measures.

But when they are asked to admit that, after the military warfare is concluded and " peace " is made, it will be desirable to have in being for future " defence " against the power of Germany an elaborate tariff, confirming and continuing the several political and military cleavages which the war has brought about, and that this tariff should be prepared during the war, they ought to apply close tests of reason before giving their assent to such proposals. What is the value of the suggested opposition between " Opulence " and " Defence "? A tariff will certainly reduce Opulence. But will it improve Defence ? And are not safer and better economic defences available ? These are the questions to be answered.

Let it be admitted that, if a nation has to choose between Opulence and Defence, it will do well to prefer the latter. But we must first have evidence that the opposition exists and that the choice is necessary. Regarded *prima facie*, Opulence is favourable, not adverse, to Defence. Poverty is not strength. Money is the sinews of war, as we, better than any other country, ought to know. If, therefore, we are to follow a course which reduces Opulence, we must be clear that this *prima facie* damage is more than offset by other items of Defence.

What are the dangers after the war against which a tariff will provide ? Needless to dwell upon the preposterous story of the huge stocks of goods (£300,000,000 in value, an adventurous statistician calculates !) which German manufacturers and merchants have already stored for " dumping " on the markets of this country and of France directly the war is over, in order to kill any revival of our trade. How Germany can spare from the remnants of her industrial population the labour needed to perform this feat, what harm it would do if Germany could send in cheap stocks at a time when our stocks and those of the commercial world will be depleted, what sort of goods Germany would take in payment, and, finally, what shred of evidence exists to support the silly fable—these probings must suffice for the " dumping " argument.

A more plausible case for economic " defence " on the part of Great Britain and her Allies is made by dwelling upon the constructive and aggressive measures of trade which the Central Empires may employ. The assumption is that an unrepentant and revengeful Germany will direct all her efforts to the work of industrial recuperation and expanding trade with three related objects: first, the recovery of her internal economic strength in order to be rich enough to prepare for another war ; secondly, the commercial and financial penetration of foreign countries, including our Empire, so as to wrest from us our trade supremacy; thirdly, the establishment at home or abroad of monopolies of certain sources of supply or processes essential for war purposes or for the control of vital industries.

In order to meet this aggressive policy we are to set up a tariff which shall (1) make Great Britain less dependent than formerly on outside supplies in war and peace; (2) bind the Empire in a closer economic unity; (3) so strengthen the trade and financial relations among the Allies as to make the Alliance a virtually self-sufficing economic system; (4) boycott the trade of the Central Powers. It is right to add that a tariff is not to be the sole instrument of economic defence. It is to be supported by navigation laws, reforms of the Company and Patents Acts, and a complete Stock Exchange boycott, etc.

But the tariff is the main weapon. Now, its defensive efficacy may be submitted to two tests. Does it strengthen the position of this country in the event of another war? Does it render less likely or more likely the occurrence of another war?

Let us here consider the first test.

Will the operation of such a tariff as is contemplated injure the power of Germany to pursue the aggressive economic policy imputed to her? She desires to build up strong internal industries, to push for foreign markets and a part in the development of backward countries, and for the possession or control of "key" industries. Now, it is evident that, if she could be cut off from all trade and other economic relations with this country, our Empire, and the dominions of our Allies, a large part of the world would be closed to her, and she would suffer. But would the general injury inflicted on her home industry and her foreign trade, and so upon the general growth of wealth of the German nation, be an advantage either to this country or to the Alliance for purposes of defence? Surely not, if it weakens us as much as it weakens our potential enemy.

And is it not a just assumption that the stoppage of trade between two nations, or groups of nations, injures or weakens both equally ? I know that there are those who think that in the past the Germans have gained more from trade with us than we have from trade with them. By this they generally mean that our imports from Germany were much larger than our exports to Germany. In 1913 did we not receive from Germany goods to the value of 80 millions, whereas we sold to Germany only 40 millions of British produce and 20 millions of colonial and foreign ? There exists a curious belief that Germany got the advantage of us in this transaction. The presumption surely ought to be the other way. For if we had really received 80 millions' worth of goods, and paid in return no more than 60 millions' worth, the "pull" would surely have been ours. In point of fact, of course, we paid in exports of goods or services, either directly to Germany or to other countries on her behalf, the full 80 millions. Apart from this necessity of trade balance, there is no ground for the belief that, because Germany sells us directly more than she buys from us, she is the greater gainer. Our Protectionists speak of our " foolish generosity " in opening our markets to our enemy, who has built up her commercial prosperity upon our amiable weakness! But has any business firm or individual trader in this country bought from Germany except for his own gain? It never occurred to him that he was acting generously because he was buying where he reckoned to get the best value. The notion that export trade is worth more than import trade is nothing but a false exaggeration of the producer's standpoint.

Another form of the same error is contained in the belief that it would injure the Central Powers much more to be cut off from trade with the British Empire and the entire territories of the Alliance than for the latter to lose their trade with the Central Powers. This no doubt would be the case if the whole world consisted of these two economic groups. It would be easier for the Allies, with their empires, to make of themselves a wholly self-contained economic system than for the Central Powers. But this is not the real problem. It ignores the importance of the neutral world, and. the processes of " roundabout " trade. If the effect of tariff walls round Great Britain, the Empire, and the Alliance, is to make our trade relations with the neutral countries more difficult, and the trade relations of Germany with the neutral countries easier, the net result may be damaging and dangerous. Now, this is precisely what would happen. Neither the British Empire nor the larger system of the Alliance can supply all their economic needs from their own territory. They must continue to be dependent on import and export trade with neutral countries, especially in North and South America, for important foods and raw materials essential to their vital industries. Although the Empire furnishes a large share of our imported foods, more comes

from foreign countries. In 1913 we drew
65½ million hundredweight of wheat and
wheat flour from foreign countries as against
57 millions from the Empire. In some
years the Imperial contribution is much
smaller. In 1908, for instance, the simultaneous failure of crops in Australia and
India made us dependent for three-quarters
of our imports upon foreign countries. For
some raw materials of our staple trades
our dependence upon foreign countries is
absolute. Take, for example, cotton. The
Imperial supply in 1913 amounted to
only 71,915,000 pounds, as compared with
2,102,384,000 pounds from foreign sources.
But what of that, it may be said? We
shall still continue in our present amicable
trade relations with the neutral countries.
They will still buy our goods and sell us theirs
as before. But will they? One inevitable
effect of our tariff system would be to damage
our trade with the great neutral markets and
to improve the trade of Germany with them.
Two forces would co-operate to this result.

German manufacturers and merchants, cut off from our markets and those of our Allies, would be driven to cultivate more assiduously than before the markets left to them. To adopt the language of our Protectionists, these neutral countries would become their "dumping-grounds," and the competition of these "dumped" German goods would undersell our honest wares. But this is not the worst. The high tariff duties which we should have to put on goods from neutral countries, in order to protect our own produce and to give preferences to our Dominions and our Allies, would give grave offence to neutral countries whose goods we have always hitherto admitted free. Retaliating on our conduct, they would no longer give us most-favoured-nation's treatment. Germany, not being hampered by so complex a tariff, and being under urgent pressure to "make up to" neutrals, would clearly be in a position to negotiate trade treaties with powerful neutrals like the United States and the countries of South America upon more

favourable terms. We should, by thus turn-
ing over the neutral markets more largely
to Germany, offset any advantages which
might seem to accrue to us by setting up
the larger economic system of the Alliance
against the smaller system of Central Europe.
So far as Great Britain is concerned, we
should be jeopardizing some of the essentials
of life and trade by reducing the number of
separate sources of supply. Thus there is no
reason to suppose that an effective economic
boycott of the Central Powers after the
war, even if it could be maintained, would
injure them more than it injured us, or, in
other words, would add anything to our
relative power of "defence."

CHAPTER III

THE TANGLES OF A TARIFF

TARIFF REFORMERS of the last decade found considerable difficulty in reconciling the claims of home industries and Imperial preferences, agrarian and manufacturing interests, tariff for revenue, tariff for Protection, and tariff for retaliation. To adjust the respective interests of producers and consumers within these islands and the Empire as purchasers of foods, raw materials, semi-manufactured and fully-manufactured goods, was found by experience to require considerable dexterity. Yet this task was child's play as compared with that which awaits our New Protectionists. For upon this earlier scheme they are called upon to superimpose the new war pattern of a world made up of friends, enemies, and neutrals, and to harmonize the operations of the new and predominant needs of defence with the national and Imperial interests of the older plan.

A tariff that is good for purposes of "defence" must, it will be admitted, be framed so as to fulfil two conditions : (1) It must bind together in unity and amity the British Empire and the Allies ; (2) it must make this union self-sufficing for all the essential requisites of war and peace. Does the proposed tariff fulfil these conditions ? That tariff has to perform a more difficult task than any ever yet erected by any State. It has to discriminate between five different bodies. It has, first, to protect the industry and agriculture of the British Isles; secondly, to give preferential treatment to the Empire ; thirdly, to cement the Alliance by mutually favourable tariff treaties ; fourthly, to apply to neutral nations a general tariff; fifthly, to exclude enemy goods, or at least to secure ourselves from dependence upon enemies for anything essential.

But when once the existing war map of the world is taken as the directive instrument for our future commercial policy, there is no tendency to confine our tariff to this fivefold discrimination. So we find proposals to distinguish friendly from unfriendly neutrals. Friendliness, again, may be either in conduct as war neutrals, or in ordinary trade relations before the war. Mr. Wickham Steed, for example, would have this country and the Allies discriminate between " first-class " and " second-class " neutrals on the basis of their favourable or unfavourable attitude during the war. " States which have clandestinely sided with and helped the enemy, or have deliberately hampered the Allies during the war ; peoples who, while able to defend themselves against eventual German aggression, have yet believed and wished for the success of German arms, must be regarded as second-class neutrals."* But I observe that the draft

* " A Programme for Peace," *Edinburgh Review,* April, 1916, p. 378.

tariff prepared by the Committee of the
London Chamber of Commerce would discriminate in the tariff treatment between
" Friendly Neutrals (giving the United
Kingdom most-favoured treatment) " and
" Other Neutral Countries (those giving
preference to other foreign countries)." Nor
is there any reason why the discrimination
should stop here.   Some neutral trade is
more important for us than other neutral
trade, irrespective of the favourable or unfavourable attitude such neutral Governments may adopt.   Here is another basis
of discrimination.

But if we apply these distinctions to
neutrals, why not also to enemy countries ?
Not only do we desire more earnestly to
damage the trade of Germany than that of
Hungary, Bulgaria, or Turkey, but some
of the imports of foods and materials from
these countries are more valuable to us
(accepting the Protectionist scale of values)
than the manufactured goods that come

from Germany. It would evidently be advantageous to us, and disadvantageous to Germany, for us to exercise a less rigorous exclusion of imports from her allies than from herself.

Indeed, when once business is crossed with politics and military considerations, there seems no limit to the complexities of the tariff discrimination. A special tariff for every foreign country, shifting with each change in the balance of political and commercial considerations, would be the logic of the situation. Some dim perception of these complications has made our New Protectionists so shy of committing themselves to any close formal statement of their proposals, that it is not easy to be certain what they stand for. I find, however, emerging from the voluminous discussions in the *Morning Post* and the reports of Chambers of Commerce meetings a new fiscal world, which may be visualized in five concentric circles:

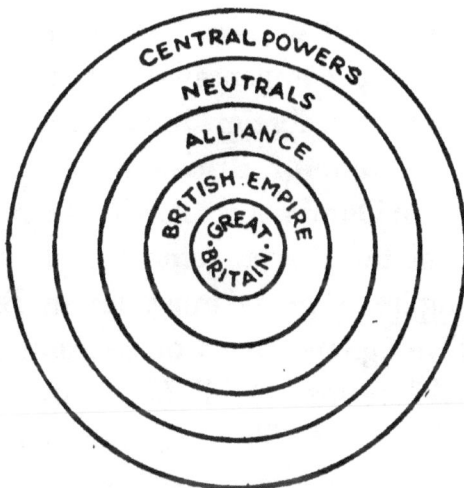

(Lent by the Strand Engraving Co.)

Now, how will it be possible to devise a
tariff that shall harmonize the conflicting
interests involved in this fivefold discrimination? The following are some of the
dangers involved in the attempt:

1. If we give adequate protection to
Great Britain, we risk offending and divid-
ing the Dominions. For the revival of
British agriculture with a view to increased
food production involves taxation of all
overseas supplies. The free market hitherto
enjoyed by foods and materials from the

Dominions will be lost. Whether this loss is or is not compensated by the higher taxation put on foreign imports, it discriminates in favour of British home producers against the Dominions. Again, if a genuinely reciprocal tariff arrangement is to " bind " the Empire, Canada must let in Bradford and Birmingham goods on genuinely " preferential " terms. Will her manufacturers consent to this? The high nominal preference originally given was soon withdrawn wherever competition with Canadian manufactures was involved. The dependence of Canada upon manufactured imports from the United States has been continually growing, and the average rates of duties on American goods are lower than on British. Will the great Free Trade movement in Western Canada acquiesce in new tariff arrangements which raise the price of agricultural machinery from the United States?

It has frequently been pointed out how exceedingly unequal must be the value to the different Dominions of any preferences accorded by this country. Canada, the richest, must gain most; the value to South Africa upon such exports as she sends must be inconsiderable.

2. The first effect of a general tariff would be to put taxes upon all the imports from our Allies that hitherto have come in free. The farmers and manufacturers of France and Belgium, in the depth of poverty and struggling to recover from the crushing effects of war, will be met by new barriers to our markets. French wines must be taxed higher, so as to favour the produce of Australia and South Africa. The embargo already placed on motors and their parts will be maintained by permanent taxes. Silks, dress goods, poultry, fruits, and flowers, will all be taxed, and it will be cold comfort to the French farmers and merchants to be told that other foreigners, who are not Allies, are charged still more.

In France considerable alarm has already been expressed in industrial and commercial circles lest they should stand to lose rather than to gain under a British post-war tariff. The following resolution, passed by the "National Association for Economic Expansion," recently formed under the leadership of M. David-Mennet, President of the Paris Chamber of Commerce, deserves attention:

"Great Britain constitutes our principal market; and British public opinion, moved by lively Press polemics, seems, at least to some extent, to incline toward Protectionist tendencies. The National Association thinks that it is urgent, in regard to the British Unionist thesis, to formulate the desiderata of France, and to show clearly that, while our sacrifices in the common struggle give us special rights, the interest of England, which buys only to sell again a half of the produce she takes from us, suggests that she should not set up against that produce a barrier which might divert it into more benevolent channels."*

The same reasoning applies to Russia. The large supplies of grain from Russia

* Quoted in *Daily Chronicle*, June 9, 1916.

must be taxed high enough to give protection to British farmers and preference to the Dominions. And this at a time when, as a faithful member of the Alliance, she is invited to abandon her trade with Germany, her largest and most profitable customer, who took one-third of her total exports. How unlikely it is that Russia will assent to such proposals appears from the recent discussion of the National Agricultural Congress at Petrograd, when the Chief of the Ministry of Trade dwelt on the utter impracticability of setting up barriers on trade with Germany.

The dependence of Russia upon Germany for a market for her surplus foods and raw materials is a "law of nature." It is based upon the permanent facts of conterminous frontiers and diversity of natural resources and economic development. Western Russia cannot dispense with German markets either for import or for export trade. Here is what M. Boublikoff, a financial expert and a member of the Duma, said at the Congress on the subject of the proposed boycott of Germany:

" Why did Russia buy so much merchandise in Germany ?   Because she was able to get it at a lower price or on more advantageous conditions than in England or in France.   It is clear, then, that the cessation of commercial relations with Germany is equivalent for the Russian consumer to an increase of the cost of living and an aggravation of the position of Russian credit.   Is impoverished Russia able to bear such a burden ?   There cannot be two answers to that question."

Such proposals are hardly likely to conduce to mutual good-will among the Allies, or the endurance of the Alliance after the immediate emergency of war has passed.

3. Nor would the trouble be confined to our Allies.

The establishment of a new complex tariff, to operate immediately peace was restored, would have a disastrous effect in retarding the recovery of our industry and commerce. At a time when, in any case, great un-

certainty must prevail as to the future
course of trade, and when business men are
gravely hampered in their plans and their
finance, this violent dislocation is to be
brought about in the delicate mechanism
of international trade.

There is not a trade in England that
would not be affected injuriously in some
way by the complications of such a tariff.

The term "key-industry" has recently
been invented to describe trades which, like
the aniline dye trade, are supports of great
staple industries. The suggestion is that a
small number of these "key-industries" exist
which at all costs must be kept under British
control. Now, this account of industry is
quite illusory. There is no important trade
which is not dependent for its successful
conduct upon dozens of other trades, many
of them necessarily outside the limits of our
country, our Empire, or the Alliance. In
the future, as in the past, we shall have to
draw many of our raw materials from foreign
countries, which might become our enemies,

or where the sources of supply might pass under enemy control. Nor can we insure that all the plant and machinery and the processes we find it best to use in our great staple industries are home-produced. Yet most of the trades producing these materials or plant or conducting these processes are "key-industries" in the sense that they are indispensable to the final product. To hold that, by tariffs or other political instruments, we can root out permanently all dependence of our necessary trades upon some product or process of foreign industry is a sheer absurdity. And if we could, we should not really fulfil the requirements of "defence." For the history even of the last few decades shows how easily new enemies may arise, how quickly such "key-industries" change, and how feeble are war alliances as securities for future amity. The new doctrine that we must keep all "key-industries" in our own hands is an impossible doctrine for any thickly peopled and highly developed country. It is only made plausible by

giving a wholly false limitation to the term
"key-industry."

4. So far as the object of our New Protection is to damage German trade by refusing
admission to our markets, it is clearly un-
attainable. Prohibitive or high tariffs can,
of course, preclude direct German imports.
But it will be very difficult to extend this
prohibition to German goods imported
through neutral countries. In respect of
many kinds of goods it will be easy to
cancel or to disguise their place of origin,
when it is the interest of the neutral country
to encourage such deceit, and of the British
importer to connive at the deceit. Large
quantities of German goods, we may be
sure, would find their way into our markets
via Belgium and Holland, Sweden, Switzerland, and Spain. They would simply cost
us extra carriage and the profits of another
middleman.

Even supposing that our regulations were
so stringent as to enable us to detect and to
exclude goods of German origin coming

through other foreign countries, the injury
inflicted by this process on German export
export trade and the protection afforded to
our manufacturers would be inconsiderable.
The German sugar, cottons, woollens, steel
manufactures, and toys, which we refused to
take from Germany, would find a larger
market in other European countries, dis-
placing their own goods for consumption
in those countries and diverting them into
our markets. What difference would it
make if, instead of receiving German engines,
Holland received those engines, and we
imported Dutch engines?

Of course, the actual effects of an attempted
boycott of German goods would be a good
deal more complicated. German semi-
manufactured goods would go to other
countries for a final process qualifying them
for entrance to our markets. Neutral
countries, profiting by the larger importation
of German steel, dyes, yarns, machinery,
chemicals, etc., which were refused entrance
to our markets, would build up manufac-

tures upon a better or cheaper basis than ours, and would out-compete our merchants in the South American or China trade.

The following list of chief staple imports from Germany into the United Kingdom in 1913 will show to what a large extent that trade consisted of goods which were raw materials or instruments of production in British manufactures, affecting the cost of production and prices of final commodities.

Staple Imports into United Kingdom from Germany.

	£
Sugar	10,912,018
Glass and manufactures... ...	1,298,384
Cottons and yarns	7,540,867
Woollens and yarns	2,592,925
Iron and steel and manufactures	7,524,533
Machinery	2,384,142
Toys	1,183,703

Since there is no *primâ facie* reason for believing that Germans gained more by selling us these goods than we from buying goods which we presumably found better or cheaper than we could get elsewhere, why is the stoppage of this trade likely to injure

4

German trade more than British trade?
How will it advantage this country to limit
its sources of supply of sugar and yarns and
machinery and chemicals, and to pay a
higher price for them ? For the notion
that we can produce all these things, as well
and as cheaply, within this country or the
Empire, without the necessity of importing
them from foreign countries, is unwarranted.
It is based upon a childish refusal to admit
the utility of specialization, division of
labour, and exchange between nations.

There is no reason for supposing that the
fivefold discrimination of the proposed tariff
would assist the " defence " of this country,
though it would certainly diminish its opulence.

No tariff could go any appreciable dis-
tance towards making the United Kingdom
economically self-sufficing for the necessaries
of life.

Exclusive dependence on our overseas
dominions for foods and other necessaries
would not reduce the submarine or other

risks in time of war, while it would, by limiting the sources of supply in time of peace, cause grave fluctuations in supplies and prices.   A tariff involving a withdrawal from our Allies of their hitherto free market in this country would operate, not as a cement, but as a dissolvent of friendship. Nor would the stiff taxation upon neutrals, necessary to furnish three lower scales of preference, conciliate the commercial or political friendship of these countries. Finally, considered as a weapon against Germany, a trade boycott, so far as it is not futile, has a recoil equal to the force of its discharge.

CHAPTER IV

PROTECTION NO DEFENCE

THE Report of the Paris Economic Conference represented the Empires of Central Europe as "to-day preparing in concert with their allies a contest in the economic plane which will not only survive the re-establishment of peace, but will at that moment attain its full scope and intensity."

In a recent interview with a representative of the United Press of America, Mr. Runciman is reported to have said : " Germany has announced that at the conclusion of the war she will attempt to establish a Customs Union of the Central Powers on aggressive lines." The general idea appears to be that Austro-Hungary should allow German science, business enterprise, and finance to develop and organize its natural resources and its industry, so as to make the Central Powers practically self-sufficing in the essentials of economic life. Joint political and economic pressure would then be used not only to bring their present allies, Bulgaria and Turkey, within this Customs Union, but to˙ persuade or coerce the smaller neutral neighbours, such as Holland, Denmark, Switzerland, perhaps Sweden, to come into a Middle European system which would divide the Western Allies from Russia and constitute the basis for a formidable political and military alliance. There is no evidence that any such plan has gone further than the pre-liminary stage of a conference between politicians and economists at Berlin and Vienna. The difficulties of the first step in so ambitious a design, a Customs Union of the two Empires, are believed by many to be insurmountable. But, assuming that Germany did throw her energies into this aggressive project, using all her diplomatic and economic resources thus to extend her business control, in order to strengthen herself for another war of conquest, would a tariff be of any use to us, either for stopping the execution of the project or for assisting us to meet its menace ?

Tariff arrangements among the Allies for the virtual boycott of the Central Powers, so far from hindering the formation of this " Middle Europe," would do everything to help it. Its advocates are already pressing upon its opponents the same argument which our Protectionists urge, viz., the need for an economic union of " defence " against the economic war we propose to wage. If we announced prohibitive duties on German-Austrian goods, with accompanying restrictions upon shipping, finance, and other economic intercourse, an immense incentive would be given to the accomplishment of the German scheme. Deprived of so large a section of the world-market, these nations would be forced partly into better organization of their common resources, partly into stronger pressure upon neutral markets both in Europe and elsewhere. Since the nature of our tariff, with its preferences to Dominions and Allies, would compel us to make stiff terms for neutrals, the countries against which we raised these new barriers would by stress of legitimate self-interest be brought over to the Central European system. Our traders complain of the ever keener competition of the Germans in the growing markets of the Far East and of South America. A tariff upon wheat from Argentina, or tea and rice from China, would hardly help us to push in these countries our manufactured goods, which would then be offered at higher prices to cover the enhanced cost of production which our general tariff would involve.

A protective tariff here can do nothing to check or impede German economic aggression. It can only make it more successfully aggressive. Would it, on the other hand, strengthen our national resistance to this aggression? How should it?

It can have only two chief and inevitable effects.

1. It would reduce our aggregate national income, and so our resources alike for armed defence upon the one hand, economic defence upon the other. How can the advocates of a policy which diminishes our funds alike for education, scientific experimentation, and technical equipment (the supreme needs for successful competition with Germany) plead " defence " ?

2. It wastes the sources of public revenue. A large proportion of the gross yield of a tariff is consumed in expenses of collection. By enabling protected industries to raise their prices it throws on consumers a burden of payment vastly greater than the gain to public revenue. The incidence of this burden is heaviest on the poorer working classes, for the prices of the necessaries of life are subject to the greatest increase. Thus the standard of living of the workers is depressed and their productive efficiency impaired.

It thus appears how bad a weapon of defence a general tariff is. But it has an even worse defect. No other policy could do so much to make another early war inevitable. The superficial notion that by hindering the economic recuperation and the commercial development of the Central Powers it would cripple their projects of "revenge" will bear no investigation. It could have no such tendency. The announcement of the intention of the Allies to pursue a punitive economic policy after the war must confirm the false statements made in Germany that England in making war was actuated by feelings of commercial jealousy. This would feed the spirit of hate and revenge, and would help to maintain in Germany the Prussian militarism we are seeking to crush. This militarism would animate the new economic system of "Middle Europe." Tariff wars would keep alive everywhere the memories of the military struggle, and would be recognized as preparations and incentives to an early renewal of the struggle, as soon as one of the two parties found a "favourable" opportunity. The "balance of power" policy in the economic world would be clearly understood to be an instrument and an index of the terrible military struggle waiting in the background. Not only Europe but the whole world would tend to be drawn into the new battle-array, as members of one economic group or the other. A breaking of Europe into two hostile commercial systems would be an even greater crime against civilization than the war itself. For it would be an open-eyed prostitution of peaceful commerce to the purposes of international hostility. It would be the perpetuation of a trench warfare in which Custom officers would take the place of soldiers. The mode of fighting would be different, the aim and the animating principle would be the same. The net effect would be to reverse the great and fruitful processes of human co-operation, not only in the mutually profitable interchange of goods, but in every other mode of intercourse. International law, so much battered and enfeebled by the experiences of war, would be unable to raise its head again in such an atmosphere, or to begin to recover that authority which is indispensable to any hope for European civilization.   All that elaborate and delicate network of communications by which, not only for business and personal relations, but for the common tasks of humanity in the world of thought and science, art, literature, and philanthropy, men of all nations have laboured together regardless of political boundaries, would suffer wreckage by this subversive enterprise.

CHAPTER V

NAVIGATION LAWS

So far I have dealt with tariffs as the weapon of defence and of offence by which our New Protectionists propose to wage "the war after the war." But there are other supplementary weapons which most of them, in concert with our Allies, desire to employ.

Supposing it be impracticable or undesirable to impose an absolute boycott on all German or other Central European goods seeking entrance to our markets, admission under a high tariff being preferable, there are various ways of hampering such trade and confining it to things that are both safe and indispensable. German commercial travellers can be penalized in the Allied countries ; German firms can be refused the protection of our Patent Laws, and can be excluded from competition for contracts. Let German capital be refused the right to "invade" the business companies of the Allied countries; let German companies, or German-owned companies of other countries, be refused quotation upon any Allied Bourse. So it would be possible to "extirpate the cancer of German trade" from our system. But, further, an organized attack can be made upon the foreign trade of Germany, not merely in all Allied markets, by discriminating harbour dues and other hampering conditions, but by adopting various methods of attack on German shipping. Why not refuse to admit into our ports all German ships, or to allow them coaling facilities, whether they carry German goods or neutral goods? Why not "keep British trade for British ships"? or, by the broader doctrine, Allied trade for Allied ships? Some of these proposals ingratiate themselves not only with avowed Protectionists, but with some nominal Free Traders. All,

however, are subject to the two defects
which we saw were fatal to tariffs as methods
of defence—the defect that the recoil is
equal to the blow for offence, and the related
defect that "two can play at that game."
If we make it more difficult for Germans to
sell their better or cheaper articles in this
country, we compel our own people to buy
and to consume dearer or worse articles.
If we refuse to admit tenders from German
firms for advertised contracts, we restrict
competition, increase the probability of col-
lusion between British contractors, compel
ourselves to pay more, wait longer, or get
inferior work.   If we deny Patent Law
protection, the same results ensue: either
we do not get the special articles our people
want, or we get them indirectly and with
greater difficulty at a higher cost.   If the
articles we thus penalize are materials,
machines, or processes serviceable to some
British industry, as is the case with many
German specialities, such as electrical and
scientific instruments, dyes and chemicals,

steel, etc., we load these British industries with some increased cost, or some inferiority of production, so hampering them for competition in export trade, and even for competition in our own markets with articles imported from foreign countries that take advantage of the superior German methods. Suppose, as is most likely, no efforts enable us to make aniline dyes as well or as cheaply as long years of scientific practice and business organization have enabled German firms to make them, our coloured textiles will compete in all foreign markets at a definite disadvantage, not merely with German goods, but with the goods of other foreign countries, such as the United States, admitting German dyes. Why should we force our consumers and our business men to buy at a disadvantage in order to injure German sellers?

No doubt it seems at first sight as if Germany could not hit back with equal force, our Imperial (and Allied) markets being so much more important to their traders than are their narrower markets to ours. But the considerations just urged prove the fallaciousness of this assumption. For the back-stroke of our boycott against German goods will be, not merely that we lose the German markets for our goods, but that we are seriously damaged in all the neutral markets of the world. This, we have already seen, will be the natural and necessary consequence of a protective tariff against the Central Powers. The further penalties we are here considering will materially enhance this damage to our neutral markets.

The proposal to exclude German ships from all British and Allied ports and coaling stations, comes with a powerful appeal to many who regard a protective tariff as a foolish or a highly questionable expedient. The abominable outrages committed by German vessels upon the high seas during the war, would, it may well appear, be appropriately punished by such a policy of exclusion. Moreover, obvious considerations of national defence appear to favour a proposal which will, by crippling the German mercantile marine, deal a damaging blow to her sea-power. A Navigation Act, therefore, takes a prominent place in the New Protectionism.

In considering the value of a navigation boycott in its bearing upon British commerce and British defence, we are fortunate in having a clearer testimony from the pages of history than is usually attainable. For early in the rise of British sea-power and foreign commerce we conducted a noteworthy experiment along these very lines. The rise of British colonial power in the seventeenth century induced our Government to lend assistance to our trading and shipping businesses in their efforts to break the pre-eminence, in some quarters the monopoly, of the carrying trade enjoyed by the Dutch. An Order in Council of 1646-47 prohibited the " plantations " from shipping any of their produce except in English bottoms. This was followed by the

fuller policy of the Navigation Act of 1651.
" It provided that no produce of any country
in Asia, Africa, or America, should be imported into any territory of the Common-
wealth save in vessels owned by Englishmen
or inhabitants of English Colonies, and
manned by crews of which more than half
were of British nationality; while the produce of any part of Europe was to be
imported only in English vessels or in vessels
owned in the country in which it was pro-
duced or manufactured."*   A few years later
the Act was further strengthened by provisions confining colonial import and export
trade to English and colonial ships of which
the master and three-fourths of the crew
were English, the same conditions being
applied to home imports of all non-European
produce and to our coasting trade.   In 1661
it was enacted that English recognition
should be confined to ships built in England.

* " Shipping after the War," by the Right Hon.
J. M. Robertson: a complete historical and economic
exposure of the " navigation " policy.

While admitting that " The Act of Navigation is not favourable to foreign commerce or to the growth of that opulence which can arise from it," Adam Smith contended that it was advantageous as a defence against the naval power of Holland. " As defence, however, is of much more importance than opulence, the Act of Navigation is perhaps the wisest of all the commercial regulations of England." It is clear, however, that the Act was primarily designed, not, as Adam Smith alleged, against Holland's naval power, but against her carrying trade and commerce. Mr. J. M. Robertson, in the pamphlet from which we have already quoted, cites ample testimony both from contemporary writers and from later historians to show that the Act had no more value for defence than for opulence. The following is his summary of the results of the actual working of these Acts :

" 1. In so far as they were specially aimed at Holland, they were certainly planned to divert carrying trade from her to England, not as a military menace.

" 2. Their real effect was to hamper English trade in all directions, one of the first results being a serious increase in prices and in the cost of shipbuilding. From twenty to ninety years after the passing of the first, English writers lament continued English inferiority to Holland in shipping and commerce.

" 3. Failing alike to promote English shipping and to depress Dutch, they obviously added nothing to English *naval* power as against Holland.

" 4. We have express English testimonies to the operation of superior Dutch *power*, in addition to supremacy in trade, many years after the first enactment; and it was after it had run for twenty-two years that the Dutch raided the Medway.

" 5. In particular, the main fields to be cultivated for the furnishing of seamen, the fisheries, were in no way improved by the monopoly policy, and seem to have been positively depressed by it. ' The numbers employed in Holland by their fishery is prodigious,' writes Harrison in 1744 (p. 24). ' I fear ours bear no comparison.'

" 6. Even the trade between Holland and England soon developed anew by way of systematic smuggling, which defrauded the English revenue. And the provision against imports of non-national produce by foreign ships seems to have set the Dutch upon extending their manufactures. Thus, a French writer on Dutch trade in 1700, referring to the English Act of 1651, states that the Dutch 'had not then anything like the manufactures they have at this moment.' "*

But if history is not encouraging to the project of reviving Navigation Acts, consideration of the economic results likely to follow from a new experiment along these lines is still more unfavourable. The first obvious effect of excluding German ships from our ports will be that British ships will be excluded from German ports. Now, since the British tonnage entering German ports before the war was about four times as great as the German shipping entering British ports, this first effect of a mutual boycott would be to our disadvantage. The next effect would be to put all the trade

* " Shipping after the War," pp. 19, 20.

which might still be carried on between Germany and Great Britain, or between the Central Powers and the Alliance, into the hands of neutral countries. Holland, Sweden, and the new mercantile marine of the United States, would be the gainers. Nor would this gain to neutrals be confined to this trade between the two hostile systems. Shipowners in Germany and in Great Britain wishing to engage in the general carrying trade of the world would find the ships carrying their national flag hampered in their most profitable use by these Navigation Laws. Ships carrying neutral flags would enjoy a great advantage. They would thus be impelled to put their ships under neutral flags, and to become investors in neutral shipping companies. Germany would certainly be disposed to take this course, both in order to reap the greater profits earned under neutral flags and their greater " freedom of the sea," and to secure immunity from capture in the event of another war.

It is, of course, possible that we might try to meet this German shipping policy by excluding from our ports neutral ships of German origin, or belonging to companies owned entirely or in large part by Germans. But how can we obtain satisfactory evidence of the ownership of every vessel claiming to enter our ports under a neutral flag? Is every foreign Government likely to obey our behest to give us an official certification of the ownership of every ship which is empowered to fly its colours, including an up-to-date list of the holders of all shares in shipping companies registered in their country? Anyone acquainted with the intricacies of modern finance, with its complication of Trust Companies and Holding Companies, will recognize the absurdity of such a notion. The mad logic of such a navigation policy would, if followed to its end, drive us to exclude on reasonable suspicion all foreign shipping, neutral as well as hostile, and to establish an all-British shipping policy.

Considering our growing national dependence upon large, free, quick, reliable sea-
transport for the existence of our population
and our industry, it would appear singularly
unwise to jeopardize our practical control
over the sea, even if we could thereby inflict
a graver injury to German commerce and
sea-power.   To take such a course after the
experience of a war in which not only the
safety, but the financial stability, of our
nation is seen so patently to rest upon our
predominance in shipping would be an act
of inconceivable folly.

CHAPTER VI

HOW TO MEET TRADE AGGRESSION

MANY who reject the idea of a general tariff in this country, either for national defence or as part of a future economic war, are quite rightly disposed to consider whether steps should not be taken to prevent certain articles and processes, which are important for war purposes or for the maintenance of vital industries in this country, from passing under foreign control.

Those who apprehend an aggressive policy in the future in trade and finance on the part of our present enemies mean two different things. Sometimes they mean that these States, by subsidies and other public aids, will set themselves to establish and to foster certain industries and branches of trade abroad, in order to have a monopoly, or a

superior position, in the event of war. Sometimes they merely mean that their traders
and industrialists, backed by the banks, will
pursue a pushful policy abroad, and by skil-
ful investments or energetic touting obtain
control of important sources of supply or
markets. In the latter case the "aggression" is nothing but successful economic
competition regarded from the standpoint of
the unsuccessful competitor. Great Britain
in this sense has been, and still is, the most
aggressive of nations, pushing her successful
trade and her control of the natural resources
of foreign countries far further than her
rivals. The British control of the huge resources of Argentina, for example, is far
more complete than that of German traders
and financiers in any foreign country.

It is no doubt possible to hold that behind
all this German trade and investment stand
the German State and its militarist policy.
That the German State has kept in closer
organic relations than our State with industry and trade, both internal and foreign,

fostering and supporting it by educational policy, transport subsidies, tariff bounties, consular assistance, etc., is not a matter of dispute. The advances made by German trade and finance in all parts of the world within the last twenty years have been, however, almost entirely the results of private business enterprise. The application of chemical and physical science to the industrial arts; the training in commerce and in languages; the detailed study and cultivation of new markets; the financial assistance given, after expert inquiry, to new industrial and commercial proposals, the main causes of German commercial development, are primarily due to the intelligence, industry, and organization, of business firms operating, not for political service, but for profits.

To pretend that all this activity is in the main a screen and an instrument of Prussian State policy, aimed to penetrate all countries of the world commercially and financially, in order to convert this economic into political control, is idle vapouring, whether it proceeds from angry bagmen or from statesmen who should be "responsible." Take as a conspicuous example the following passage from a speech delivered at the opening of the Paris Conference by M. Briand :*

"The war has shown us the extent of *economic slavery* to which we were to be made subject. We must realize that the danger was great, and that *our adversaries were on the eve of success.* Then came the war. The war, with the immense sacrifices which it demands, will not have been in vain if it brings about *an economic liberation of the world,* and restores sane commercial methods. We are all determined to shake off *the yoke which was being forced upon us,* and to resume our commercial intercourse in order freely to join it to that of our Allies."

What is signified by the passages here italicized, or by corresponding language in the preamble of the Report of the Paris

* *Times* Report, June 15, 1916.

Conference? What economic slavery was
Germany seeking to impose on France, and
on the world, from which this war will
liberate them? Germans (not Germany)
were no doubt increasing the volume of
their foreign trade; their manufactures were
entering new markets in various countries.
Wealthy Germans were investing an increasing quantity of savings in mining, railroad, and industrial companies in France,
Italy, Belgium, and other European countries, as well as large sums in similar business
enterprises in the United States, South
America, and elsewhere. What of that?
In what real sense has the United States
been subject to "economic slavery" because
her business men have borrowed enormous
sums from European investors to make their
railways and open up their resources? If
some of the spare capital of Germany in
recent years has gone into French companies
engaged in developing iron and coal, does
M. Briand seriously contend that this has
injured or imposed "domination" upon

France—*i.e.*, that Frenchmen would have been better off if they had not borrowed abroad larger quantities of useful capital at lower rates than they could get at home ? In some French and Italian enterprises German investors, or even German banks, doubtless exercised a preponderant control, as British investors or financial companies do in Argentina and many other countries. But in what sense has the war exhibited these operations as "economic slavery," unless in the sense in which Socialists regard all capitalist control in this light ?

The German State has doubtless had a powerful secret service in many foreign countries, and may have utilized branches of German firms abroad as sources of political information. The widespread employment of German clerks in foreign commercial houses has undoubtedly given German firms a fuller knowledge of the business conditions of their foreign competitors than commercial firms in England possess.

But all these arts and practices are nothing

else than an intelligent seizure of legitimate
business opportunities. What German firms
have been doing, our firms also should have
been doing, and, so far as we have been
successful, have been doing. The notion
that all this expanding German trade and
finance have been the cat's-paw of the aggressive German State is baseless. The capitalists
who rule German industry, trade, and finance,
are out for profits, not for political aims, and
their success would have been impossible on
any other terms. Like business men in every
other country, they get what use they can
from the Government, in the way of education, transport, tariffs, and diplomatic pressure. But the suggestion that German
traders, bankers, colonists, are merely advance agents of the German State is one
of those impositions upon credulity which
would not have been possible in any other
atmosphere than that of war. There is no
better illustration of this credulity than the
easy acceptance by " the man in the street "
of the familiar charge against Germans of

pursuing a policy of "scientific dumping."
The only intelligible meaning to this term
would be that of a deliberate policy of a
German cartel or "monopoly" to pour goods
on to our markets at cut-prices, so as to ruin
British competitors, drive them out of trade,
and then improve their goods at prices
raised so as to recoup them for the earlier
cut-prices by which they acquired the market.
I believe a good many people believe this is
what "the Germans" have been doing. But
nobody can point to any actual trade where
they have done it. In theory, no doubt,
it is a possibility, though the conditions of
success would be very difficult. In practice
it has been found impossible to dump successfully in a Free Trade country. "It has,"
says Mr. Macrosty,* "been demonstrated by
abundant German experience that dumping
does not pay, and that it is more advantageous for a domestic trust or cartel that
export trade should be so regulated as to
yield the maximum of profit."

* "The Trust Movement in British Industry," p. 342.

It is pretty safe to assume that German and other rival traders and investors are, broadly speaking, out for profit, and for profit only, and that they place their money or their goods wherever the prospect of gain is greatest and most secure.

There may be cases, however, where private business or scientific enterprise has made some discovery, or opened up some trade, which has a special political or military value. An instance would be that of the metal tungsten, used for hardening steel, the bulk of the sources of which are said to have been secured by Germans. Such cases, where they can be shown to exist, might legitimately be removed from the ordinary category of trade for our present discussion, and classed with those other trades in Germany or elsewhere which are admittedly aided and encouraged by the State, in part, for military considerations. So far as any State for "aggressive" purposes directs its "national economy" in such a way as to endanger our supplies either of military

6

requisites or of any necessity of life in the
event of war, it is manifestly the duty of our
State to take whatever means are necessary
to meet such " aggression." For instance, if
it were necessary to secure ourselves against
the sudden withdrawal in war-time of the
supply of some vitally important goods in
which we were in danger of complete de-
pendency upon an enemy, it would be quite
legitimate to prohibit the entrance of such
goods, provided that we were able to establish
a domestic substitute under conditions which
were not those of an ordinary " protected "
trade. There are various ways in which
this could be done. If importation was
prohibited, the excessive profits which " protected " private businesses might make could
be checked either by Excise duties or by a
special profit tax, or by some such regulation
of prices to consumers as is attached to the
working of gas companies and other semi-
public monopolies. Or, simpler and better
still, such industries could be established and
worked as public monopolies. This would

be for various reasons the more desirable course. For, in the first place, in most if not all cases where real danger to our national defence was apprehended, the industry would relate closely to some class of armaments. Now, although in war itself it may be necessary to call upon private engineering firms to supplement the State supplies of arms, it ought clearly to be the function of the State to carry on the ordinary production of arms in its own factories and workshops, not allowing great private vested interests in war to grow up within the body of the nation. If, therefore, the aggressive trade policy of any foreign State threatens to deprive our State of articles essential for our defensive services, the production of such articles clearly falls within the proper scope of State enterprise. It is to this national organization of defensive industries, and not to tariffs, that we should look for our defence.

But outside this restricted circle of war requisites there are a number of industries producing trade materials or consumable

goods which we have "allowed" to pass pre-
dominantly or completely into foreign and
sometimes German hands. Four articles are
especially prominent in illustration of this
economic peril—dyes, monazite, tungsten,
and beet sugar. Now, an exceedingly per-
tinent commentary on these articles was
made in a letter to *The Times* of March 30
by Dr. F. A. Mason, who remarks: "The
four subjects noted — tungsten for steel-
making, monazite for the production of gas
mantles, synthetic indigo, and beet sugar—
do not appear at first sight to bear much
relation to one another, but their mention
with regard to German industrial success
and British failure is no fortuitous one. The
link connecting them all may be summed
up in one word—chemistry. There is no
branch of science, pure or applied, which has
been so shamefully neglected in the past as
chemistry. Practically all the important industries in which we have been left behind
by Germany have been those in which the
chemist is predominant." Admittedly all

the industries in which Germans are pre-
eminent are those in which science, education, and business organization, count heavily.
In order to defend ourselves, the obvious
method is to cultivate these factors of success.
Will a tariff help us here? The general and
natural tendency of Protection is to dis-
courage energy, experiment, and progress, in
technical and business methods. To decline
competition and to shirk behind a tariff
wall is not only a cowardly, but a singularly
foolish, way of meeting the superiority of
our trade rivals in certain industries. If
this superiority is built on brains, science,
and organization, we had better build our
"defence" upon the same basis. Only thus
can be got a really reliable defence. For the
most striking fact in this type of scientific
industry is that it is continually growing
and changing. The so-called "key-industry"
of to-day will not be the "key-industry" of
to-morrow. War is an eye-opener in this
matter. Sir Hugh Bell, in writing on the
subject, makes a criticism which I commend

to short-sighted Tariff " Reformers," whose instrument would be always lagging behind the real need of the nation : " Who can say what, when war is next waged by mankind, will be the 'key-industry'? Peradventure some delicate alloy of steel involving the use of a rare metal. Shall we 'protect' (heaven save the mark!) all rare metal industries, lest one of them should be found the way to the dominion of the air, as may easily be the case ?"*

Would not it be safer to set about improving our processes of education, so that we may have at least an equal chance with Germany, or any other nation, in discovering and developing new " key-industries " ?

* " Trade after the War," April, 1916.

CHAPTER VII

THE CASE OF AGRICULTURE

THERE is one great fundamental industry which deserves separate consideration in this problem of economic defence—agriculture. The belief that the decline of farming is an injurious factor in our recent history is by no means based exclusively on considerations of militarism and defence. The decay of rural industries and the concentration of our population in great cities, removed from wholesome regular contact with Nature and devoted more and more exclusively to mechanical and commercial pursuits, have been sources of deep concern for hygienic, æsthetic, and moral reasons. Those concerned for the quantity and quality of our population have pointed with alarm to the dwindling proportion of the population living in the country, where the birth-rate remains higher and the infantile mortality lower than in the towns, and where, in spite of a selective drawing of the best stock into towns, the general standard of health and longevity is higher. These general criticisms have, however, been greatly reinforced by considerations of national defence. Larger families born and bred in the country are wanted for cannon food. And the degree of our dependence upon overseas supply of food is now more than ever realized as a national danger.

It is natural, therefore, that various proposals for stimulating agriculture, keeping population on the soil, and improving the conditions of life in our villages, should be to the fore. This is no place for a general discussion of the merits of this branch of "social reform." It must suffice to note the part Protectionism is likely to play in it.

By character and tradition the landowners and farmers of this country, as of many others, are Protectionists. But at the present time they are the more incited to seek Governmental aid in the form of tariffs, bounties, remissions of rating, etc., because the recent political campaign, to which Mr. George was seeking to commit the country before the war, was causing them serious alarm. If they were to be called upon to raise agricultural wages to a decent minimum, to assist in the creation of " free " cottages, and the establishment on a large scale of small holdings, and to assent to other means of raising the independence of the labourers, they were impelled more urgently to demand from the Government some simple guarantees that their rents and profits shall not be swallowed up by these improvements of the conditions of labour. They must be secured against the incalculable inrushes of foreign foods into our markets. Prices of food must be kept at a level which will make farming possible, and give the farmers sufficient security of outlook to "do their best by the land." To keep out foreign foods is the expedient generally advocated, and though town Protectionists have learnt the lesson of the 1906 and 1910 elections, and avoid committing themselves to any sort of food tax, the landed interests are not easily shaken from their fixed policy. Though the programme of the London Chamber of Commerce allows most foods to come in free, no political Protectionism, having regard to considerations of Imperial union, would be likely to endorse this liberty. This simple claim of the farmer is likely to remain a millstone on the neck of the New Protectionism.

It would, of course, be possible to deal with the agricultural claims by way of bounties instead of tariffs. Sir L. Chiozza Money has recently revived this proposal, urging that a bounty upon agricultural produce should be applied to stimulate and organize our home supplies. Imported foods might enter free of duty as before, but a bounty on home-grown foods would

put more of our land into effective use, so
increasing the proportion of our home
supply. Some of the difficulties raised by
the bounty policy, as usually advocated, are
met by the more audacious scheme outlined
by Sir Leo,* who would make his bounties an
instrument of a general organization of our
agriculture by the State. The comparative
failure of the rising price of wheat in recent
years to stimulate an increase of the
acreage under wheat is doubtless attributable partly to the slowness of the agricultural
mind to respond to economic stimuli, partly
to the insecurity of tenure of most farmers,
partly to the fact that other food prices
have also risen, and last, not least, to the
fact that the gain from higher prices is
liable to be taken by landowners in higher
rent. If anything effective is to be done
along these lines, agriculture as a whole
must be brought under a general State
surveillance ; there must be security for the
maintenance of the higher profits of farming;

* *Westminster Gazette*, May 31, 1916.

the labourer, as well as the farmer, must get his share of agricultural prosperity.

" I picture the State as commanding the whole question of food-supply, just as it has commanded the sugar-supply in this war, and just as it has partly commanded the meat-supply in this war. My conception is that the State, having after due consideration decided to apply varying proportions of British soil to different agricultural purposes, shall buy up and control the home supply, paying to the producers such a price as will enable them to maintain themselves at a proper standard of life. The minimum wage in agriculture becomes part and parcel of the plan." " Thus controlling the British output of, let us say, grain, meat, and dairy produce, the Government would next proceed to make arrangements with the British Dominions overseas to purchase from them their surplus productions of wheat." " As to other supplies, the food surpluses of Argentina or the United States or Denmark, there is no reason why the British Government should not act similarly, or alternatively admit such foreign produce at some moderate rate of duty."

In order, therefore, to meet the obvious defects of an ordinary bounty scheme, it is proposed to establish a State monopoly in the supply of food. A State department is apparently to supersede all the present regulative motives of supply and of demand, fixing the quantity of all the different sorts of uses to which our land is to be put, and the quantity of " surpluses " of various kinds to be bought, first, from our different Dominions, and, secondly, from different foreign countries ; finally it is to control an intricate machinery of distribution in order to supply to every consumer in the country the State rations which it has been calculated he ought to be allowed to buy and to consume. For if the State organizes the supply of foods, fixing the prices it pays to the home, the colonial, and the foreign producer, and the quantities it buys from each, and fixing, on the other hand, the selling prices to the consumer (including the manufacture in the numerous food-making industries), the nation is virtually put on rations. And this not as a temporary war but as a permanent peace measure !

In a parenthetic paragraph Sir Leo expresses his belief that it would be "wise and profitable" for the State to acquire by purchase the whole of our agricultural lands. Indeed, it is tolerably obvious that, unless this step were taken, the bulk of the bounty money paid by the State for high-priced agricultural produce would pass into the hands of landlords in raised rents.

But surely it is a *reductio ad absurdum* of the "bounty" system when it is seen to require for its defence the nationalization of land and the socialization of the entire food trade of the country. For Socialists have generally and rightly recognized that agriculture is the branch of industry least adapted for direct State administration, by reason of the infinite variety of local conditions and the other irregularities of

materials and processes which render it re-
fractory to rigorous routine.   Most of those
who favour the ownership and control by the
State of railroads, mines, and the great staple
manufactures, recognize that the direct incentives of private individual gain and liberty
of working are essential to get the best out
the soil.

That the State can do much to stimulate
and improve agriculture must be admitted.
But the assistance does not lie along the
road of tariffs or bounties.   The real need
is to release agriculture from the rusty
chains of medieval land tenure, and to place
it on a modern business footing, affording
to the employer and the worker the hopes
and prospects of gain requisite to evoke
their intelligent and efficient industry.   Reform of land tenure, scientific and business
training for the farmer's son, skilled crafts-
man's wages and personal liberty for the
wage-earner (with the option of an independent livelihood upon a small holding),
improved and cheapened transport for agri-

cultural produce, local co-operative associations for marketing and for credit—these are the chief desiderata for enlarging the yield of British agriculture. The State ought to contribute liberally to these purposes—legislatively, by removing the decaying relics of feudal tenure ; administratively, by the public services of education, transport, and cheap credit.

To take money from the consuming public or from the gains of other industries in order therewith to subsidize a favoured industry of agriculture, by means of tariffs or bounties, is bad politics and worse economics.

Finally, regarded as defence, the protection of agriculture is fatally defective. Although it may theoretically be possible to show that, by a general application of modern science and intensive cultivation, a sufficient quantity of food could be raised upon our national soil to support our whole population, nobody seriously supposes that this can or will be done. The utmost that is looked for as the result of Protection or agricultural reform is some not very marked reduction of our dependence upon overseas supplies. We cannot hope, with our great and still growing population, to be able in the future to feed ourselves in the event of a war in which we might be cut off from overseas supplies. Nor will considerations of defence encourage us to rely upon the Empire for all the surplus food-supplies we shall continue to require. For statistics show that even in recent years, with the immense development of Canadian resources, the Empire does not furnish us, in ordinary years, with much more than a third of the imported foods we require. The statistics of our imports of wheat and flour* show how precarious it would be for us to rely upon Imperial resources, which in a bad year cannot supply us with more than a quarter of our needs. The large number and variety of the foreign sources of supply upon which hitherto we have been drawing are seen to be the essential conditions of a

* See table on p. 98.

7

regular and reliable food-supply for our population. Any weakening or reduction of these sources of supply, by tampering with our freedom of imports, under the pretext of Imperial union or preference for Allies, would imperil our national existence.

---

* GREAT BRITAIN'S IMPORTS OF WHEAT AND FLOUR PER CENT.

	1915.	1912.	1908.	1907.	1906.	1904.
BRITISH EMPIRE:						
Canada	23·62	21·91	16·42	13·15	11·79	7·10
India	13·53	20·53	2·70	15·81	11·22	21·60
Australia	0·18	10·40	5·35	7·36	7·57	9·62
New Zealand ...	—	0·23	—	—	0·07	0·29
Total British Empire	37·33	53·07	24·47	36·32	30·65	38·61
FOREIGN COUNTRIES:						
United States ...	49 41	20·88	36·28	28·94	32·53	16·20
Russia	0·77	7·26	4·72	9·89	14·30	20·37
Argentina	11 90	15·30	29·18	19·00	17·20	18·48
Roumania	—	0·64	1·18	2·20	2·27	0·94
France	0·09	0·45	0·46	0·87	0·81	1·88
Austro-Hungary ...	—	0·13	0·32	0·52	0·77	0·87
Bulgaria	—	0·10	0·09	0·36	0 45	0·13
Turkey	0·02	0·26	0·32	0·40	0·14	0·31
Chile	—	0·53	2·03	0·07	—	0·78
Germany	—	0·67	0·57	0·48	0·31	0·52
OTHER COUNTRIES	0·48	0·71	0·38	0·95	0·57	0·91
Total	62·67	46·93	75·53	63·68	69·35	61·39

* *Statist*, June 17, 1916.

The advantages Great Britain possesses
in her natural resources, her situation, her
internal and external means of transport,
her volume of capital, are greater than those
of Germany. It is in the intelligent organization and direction of these advantages
that we have fallen behind. Better scientific,
technical, commercial, and general education among all classes of our people, trained
intelligence in industry, is the first desider-
atum. But in order to get this use from
education we must first believe in education. Faith must precede works. This is
a hard saying for a people which has selected
for one of its few public economies in war-
time a " letting down " of all its educational services.

Our numerous colonies and protectorates
scattered over the world should give our
men of commerce an immense advantage
over other nations, as outlook towers and
vantage grounds for trade and for investments. But the modern successful trader
must learn languages, mix on terms of easy

intercourse with foreigners of different races, colours, and grades of civilization, learn their habits and material needs, and the best ways of satisfying them: he must study his potential markets in detail. If he is too proud or too indolent to do this, he will be "left" behind by Germans, Dutchmen, or Swiss, who will better conform to the requirements of the situation.

As for our complaints that the German Consulates render so much more valuable assistance to their traders than do ours, the remedy is obvious. It consists in a thorough reform of the selection, the personnel, and the work, of our Consulates. It should be their function to make a continuous organized study of commercial opportunities, to follow the industrial developments of the country, to know what public or private contracts are available for foreign competition, and to lose no time in communicating this information to the home Government for circulation in this country.

Finally, we must meet the superior

financial penetration by means of which the great German banks have operated in foreign countries, not by silly accusations of " aggression," but by intelligent imitation. Credit is the great instrument of expanding trade. We have in Great Britain a huge latent reservoir of unused or ill-used credit. Though our banks are not in their existing structure adapted to the more adventurous work done by such institutions as the Deutsche Bank in launching and financing great industrial and trading enterprises, other modes of organizing credit for such purposes are open to us. One of the revelations of the war has been that of the great national reserve of credit available in time of need for galvanizing into life the stiffening sinews of our banking and financial system, and for supporting the vast expenditure upon the war of our country and our Allies. The establishment of Credit Institutions in this country, furnished with sufficient capital to play the part taken by the German banks in initiating and maintaining new projects whose soundness has been attested by expert inquiry, is a proposition which is already commending itself to enlightened financiers. What part the joint-stock banks may take in such an institution, what part the Government, is a matter for discussion. But the utility, even the necessity, of some such organization of credit, if our commercial and investing classes are to compete on equal terms with those of Germany, is generally admitted.

When, then, we inquire what the weapons are with which Germany has made her great "invasions" in the world markets and international finance, we find that they are weapons of organization forged by brains, will, and industry, and are within our grasp if we also have the brains and will and industry to forge them. If we have not, the cowardly protection of a tariff will not serve us; for, instead of acting as a stimulus to efficiency and enterprise, it will be a screen for slackness and incompetence.

CHAPTER VIII

FREE TRADE AS A POLICY

THE attempt to discredit Free Trade as a policy which has endangered this country in time of war rests on a particularly reckless perversion of the facts. For the course of the war has shown that the staying power and fighting strength of Great Britain depend in the last resort upon our naval and mercantile supremacy at sea and our dominant position in world commerce and finance. Now, these factors are themselves the products and expressions of our Free Trade policy. Our ownership of half the shipping of the world and our control of commerce over the great world-routes could only have been developed and maintained by our policy of free ports and markets. The vital importance of our mercantile marine for transport and other subsidiary war purposes, as well as for the maintenance of necessary supplies for the needs of our civil population, requires no argument. The swift, full, and easy access to the markets of neutral countries, for the supply of the requisites of war and peace to ourselves and our Allies, has been the greatest, and will probably prove the determinant, advantage we possess over our enemies in a protracted war. This advantage is the direct outcome of Free Trade. The good-will shown to our cause by most neutral nations is not attributable entirely, as we are prone to think, to the justice of our cause or the considerateness of our conduct on the sea. To a large extent it is a half-conscious acknowledgment of the superior liberality of our commercial policy.

Not less important is the contribution of Free Trade to the financial strength that has enabled us to bear the great economic burdens of a war in which we have been able to render invaluable aid in goods and money to our Continental Allies. It is not merely that Free Trade has developed our industry and commerce on sound and profitable lines, so enriching the nation as to enable it to find for a great emergency the huge financial resources we have provided in the last two years. But the facts that London has been the financial centre for the entire world, and that the financial direction of world-commerce and of the distribution of the savings of the world has been mainly in our hands, are indissolubly connected with Free Trade. Now, this supremacy has been of incalculable value in helping us to finance the war. We have been able to draw in for our immediate needs huge liquid funds of capital laid out in financing world-commerce, and to establish relations of credit and exchange in the United States and elsewhere, resting ultimately upon our financial and commercial prestige. Should we revert to Protection, and break Europe into two rival economic systems—throwing many of the neutrals into close fiscal relations with the

Central Powers, the unquestioned supremacy of the " bill on London " would be lost, and a most injurious blow would have been inflicted on our control of world finance and commerce.   Setting on one side the general effect of such a weakening of our national resources, we cannot fail to recognize how damaging this loss would be to the cause of national defence in the event of another war.

" But, at any rate," it is sometimes said, "you must admit that Free Trade has failed as a pacific agency."   We can admit no such thing.   If the example set by this nation had been followed by the other Powers, and nevertheless this world-war had broken out, it might have been contended that Free Trade had failed.   But why does it seem even plausible to suggest that, because a number of Protectionist nations quarrel and come to blows, and Free Trade Britain is drawn in, Free Trade and not Protection has failed ?   No one who has followed recent Continental history can ignore the fact that tariff wars between Germany and Russia, Austria and Italy, and the oppressive tariff placed by Austria on Servia, have been active influences in fomenting national hostilities and in stimulating preparations for this war.

British Free Trade could not keep the world at peace.   But it has helped to keep Britain at peace.   Can anyone seriously suppose that in this dangerous world Great Britain would have been permitted to gain and to hold so huge a territorial Empire scattered over the wide world, or to wield, virtually uncontested for so long a time, the supremacy of the seas, had not the natural jealousy and envy of other Powers been abated by the freedom and equality of commerce which we gave to traders of all nations? The closer Protection and the discriminative tariffs of our self-governing dominions, taken together with the threats of a withdrawal of our free Imperial markets, are among the admitted causes of the later war-policy of Germany.   If we had claimed the most profitable fifth of the whole inhabited world for our exclusive markets, and had treated the manufacturers and traders of all other rising commercial nations as trespassers, it cannot be doubted that a combination of European nations would long ago have banded themselves against this arrogant monopoly.

Protection is not a good defence either as a normal trade policy or in war-time. If any simple test is wanted, it is furnished in the fact that as soon as the war started the great Protectionist belligerents, one after another, dropped their food tariffs. Italy reduced her duties on food in October, 1914, and abolished her corn tax in the following February. In October, 1914, Austria abolished her corn tax. In September, 1914, the German duties on bread, beans, butter, eggs, poultry, prepared foods, cereals and flour, meat and fish, were abolished. So much for the defence value of Protection in war-time! And yet these countries are comparatively self-sufficing in their food-supply. How much worse a defence would a tariff prove for us!

But if Protection fails to provide that self-sufficiency in war-time, which is its ostensible object, what shall be said of it as a method of war finance? While Great Britain by a series of increases of direct taxation, almost wholly falling upon current income has raised the revenue from a pre-war level of 175 millions to a figure estimated in 1916-17 to amount to 509 millions, what have the Protectionist nations done towards meeting their costs of war out of current revenue? Virtually nothing. The speech of Dr. Helfferich, Finance Minister for Germany, in the Reichstag, August 20, 1915, is a sufficient testimony to the helplessness of Protectionist finance to meet emergencies: " I explained in March the reasons which determined the German Government against the imposition of war taxes during the period of the war. These reasons will stand. We do not desire to increase by taxation the heavy burden which war casts upon our people, so long as it is not absolutely necessary. As things are, the only method seems to be to leave the settlement of the war-bill to the conclusion of peace and the time after peace has been concluded." In other words, Germany has been obliged to borrow every penny she has spent upon the war. Nor is that all. This year (1916), in order to meet the growing interest on the debt, Dr. Helfferich proposed taxes estimated to yield 24 millions a year. But that sum will furnish a good deal less than one-quarter of the interest of the war-borrowing actually incurred. Worse than that, closer inspection makes it evident that with this new taxation Germany will still be unable, not merely to contribute to the current costs of war, but to find the revenue required for her imperial expenditure upon an ordinary peace footing. As the Cobden Club shows in an able leaflet: " This means not only that Germany has not paid a penny out of income for the war, but that she has been obliged to borrow about half her ordinary peace expenditure as well." The same story is true of the other belligerent countries, and for the same reason. Tariffs are broken reeds for war emergencies. Countries that trust to them for revenue in wartime are foredoomed to failure. For just when more money is wanted less is supplied. In most belligerent countries import trade is heavily diminished, and with this diminution the yield of import duties falls. The rates cannot be increased at a time when restricted supplies are raising prices. On the contrary, duties upon necessaries must be reduced or repealed, as we see has actually happened. This financial defect, perilous to national defence, is inherent in a protective system. It is no mere chance that has imparted so much elasticity of revenue to our national finance. The simple reason is that, whereas in war Germany, France, Russia, Italy, rely upon indirect taxes for the great bulk of their current revenue, this country is raising 72 per cent. of her revenue by direct taxation.

Free Trade has enabled us not merely to make a considerable and growing contribution to our own current war expenditure, but to undertake the added burden of finding huge sums for the assistance of our Allies. Only by means of the immense and various commerce with foreign countries, built up by our habitual policy of free markets, by the predominant power of our navy and mercantile marine—itself at once the product and the support of our free markets—and by the vast resources of credit and financial machinery established for the conduct of this commerce, could Great Britain have made what will prove to be the determinant· contribution to the resistance by which the superior military preparations of Germany will be worn down.

CHAPTER IX

THE OPEN DOOR

So far I have discussed the New Protectionism as a complicated form of folly. But it is more than that. It is a crime—I had almost written *the* crime — against civilization. For its effect, as its intention, would be to perpetuate the present strife by stamping the divisions made for war upon the world of commerce afterwards. Whereas the whole trend of civilization has been to bind the peoples of the world into closer unity of interests and activities by the growing interdependence of commerce, these proposals are directed to a reversal of the movement. Not merely do they seek to cut across the whole delicate network of commercial and human intercourse, but they make precisely that severance which is most injurious to the future of humanity. To break Europe into two hostile and rival economic bodies, intriguing against one another in all the neutral countries. of the world, would be to endow with permanency the political system of contending alliances, which has been the chief cause of past insecurity. This political antagonism would be loaded with economic interests which, once established, would be very difficult to displace. The question of the just deserts of Germany and the desire to impose upon her economic punishment are not a real issue. For we have seen that the constitution and working of modern commerce are such as to disable Protection, or other modes of commercial severance, from inflicting any injury which does not equally recoil upon the party inflicting it. Nor are the private sensibilities and animosities of Britons who desire to have no commercial dealings in the future with Germany in question. No trading firm or individual in this country is precluded from putting into operation on his own behalf a complete boycott of German goods. It is his desire to impose his policy upon other firms and other persons, who may still wish to seek their advantage by buying and selling in the best market that is in question.

The adoption of a State policy which, by stopping all healing intercourse between the members of the belligerent groups, would keep alive and exacerbate all the bitterest memories of war, would be nothing short of treason against the cause of civilization. For commerce has always been the greatest civilizer of mankind. All other fruits of civilization have travelled along trade routes. The caravans which crossed the great Asiatic plains, the boats which conducted the earliest commerce up and down the great river courses, carried the first seeds of science, religion, art, law, and of mutual understanding and good-will, among ever-widening circles of mankind. Cut off commerce, and you destroy every mode of higher intercourse. Substitute commercial war for free exchange, and you reverse the current of all civilization and drive back to barbarism.

The full pacific virtues of Free Trade and the constructive policy which it requires have seldom yet been recognized, even by professed Free Traders. This is due to a failure fully to appreciate the profound change that has come about in the economic internationalism of the last half-century. Trade, in its simple meaning of exchange of goods for goods, does not cover the new industrial, commercial, and financial relations between members of different countries. Cobden was admittedly mistaken in thinking that the perception of their obvious self-interest must rapidly lead all other nations in the world to liberate their trade as we had done, and that this universal Free Trade would afford security against future war. His error lay in failing to perceive that, though the interest of each people as a whole lay in freedom of commerce, the interests of special groups of traders or producers within each country would continue

to lie along the lines of privilege and protection, and that until democracy became
a political reality these organized group
interests might continue to mould the fiscal
policy of their several States.

But though this consideration has retarded
the pacific influence of commerce, it has not
been a direct and potent influence for international dissension. While the refusal of
nations to open their markets on equal
terms to foreigners retards and chills friendship, it does not normally promote hostility.
It is the struggle for colonies, protectorates,
and concessions in undeveloped countries,
that has been the most disturbing feature
in modern politics and economics. Foreign
policy in recent decades has more and more
turned upon the acquisition of business advantages in backward parts of the world,
spheres of commerce, influence, and exploitation, leases, concessions, and other privileges,
partly for commerce, but mainly for the
profitable investment of capital. For it is
the export of capital, the wider and more

adventurous overflow of the savings of the capitalists of the developed Western countries, that constitutes the new and dominant factor in the modern situation. Larger and larger quantities of capital are available for overseas investment, and powerful, highly organized firms and groups of financiers seek to plant out these savings in distant lands, where they can be loaned to spendthrift monarchs or ambitious Governments, or applied to build railways, harbours, or other public works, to open and work mines, plant tea, rubber, or sugar, or to serve the general money-lending operations which pass under the name of banking. Many hundreds of millions of pounds during recent years have been flowing from the creditor nations of Europe into this work of "development," which forms the main material ingredient in what is sometimes called the "march," sometimes the "mission," of civilization among backward peoples.

It is the competition between groups of

business men, financiers, and traders, in the
several nations, using the offices of their
respective Governments to assist them in
promoting these profitable business enterprises, that has underlain most of the
friction in modern diplomacy and foreign
policy, and has brought powerful nations
so often into dangerous conflict. To
prove this statement, one has only to name
the countries which have been the recent
danger-areas : Egypt, Morocco, Tripoli,
Transvaal, Persia, Mexico, China, the Balkans. Though in every case other considerations, racial, political, dynastic, or religious,
are also involved, sometimes more potent in
the passions they evoke, the moving and
directing influences have come from traders,
financiers, and bondholders. Through the en-
tanglements of Anglo-French political policy
in Egypt runs the clear, determinant streak
of bondholding interests. The kernel of the
Moroccan trouble was the competition of
the Mannesmann and the Schneider firms
over the "·richest iron ores in the world."

Mining financiers moulded the policy of South Africa towards annexation of the gold reef. Tripoli was in essence a gigantic business coup of the Banco di Roma. In Mexico history will find a leading clue to recent disturbances in the contest of two commercial potentates for the control of oil-fields. Persia came into modern politics as an arena of struggle between Russian and British bankers, seeking areas of profitable concessions and spheres of financial influence. In China it was the competition for railroads and for leases and concessions, followed by forced pressures, now competing, now combining to plant profitable loans. Turkey and the Balkans became an incendiary issue to Western Europe because they lay along the route of German economic penetration in Asia, a project fatally antagonized by Russian needs for " free " Southern waters.

The pressure of demand from organized business interests for preferential economic opportunities in backward countries is the driving force behind the grievances and aspirations of thwarted nationalism, political ambition, and imperialistic megalomania. A recent writer* has thus condensed these facts of history: "It is essential to remember that what turns a territory into a diplomatic problem is the combination of natural resources, cheap labour, markets, defencelessness, corrupt and inefficient government."

If the Free Trade policy is to fulfil its mission as a civilizing, pacifying agency, it must adapt itself to the larger needs of this modern situation. Free Trade is indeed the nucleus of the larger constructive economic internationalism; but it needs a conversion from the negative conception of *laissez faire*, *laissez aller*, to a positive constructive one. The required policy must direct itself to secure economic liberty and equality not for trade alone, but for the capital, the enterprise, and the labour, which are required to do the work of development in all the backward countries of the earth, whether those coun-

* Mr. Lippmann, " The Stakes of Diplomacy," p. 93.

tries "belong to" some civilized State or are as yet independent countries. This fuller doctrine of the Open Door, or equality of economic opportunity, cannot, however, be applied without definite co-operative action on the part of nations and their Governments.

This needs plain recognition. For to some who have perceived the dangerous diplomatic emergencies arising from the support given by Governments to the private business ventures of their nationals it has appeared the easiest escape to advocate a doctrine of mere political disinterestedness. Let Governments give their traders, investors, and financiers, to understand that, while they are at liberty to enter any business relations they like with the members or the Governments of other nations, they are not empowered to call upon their Government for assistance, either in establishing or pushing such business, or in redressing any injuries which may be done to them or their property interests. Such business, unauthorized by Government

and undertaken for private profit, must carry
its own risks.   Why, it is asked, should
persons who have staked their property
in countries where they know the Government to be corrupt, the administration of
law to be uncertain, the treatment of
foreigners to be unjust, and who presumably
have discounted these very risks in the
terms of their investments or their trade,
be at liberty to call upon their Governments
to use the public resources of their country to
rescue them from these risks and to improve
the value of these private speculations? The
logic of this attitude appears irrefutable.
But the politics are utterly unpractical and
inconsistent with humanitarian progress.
No Government has ever maintained, or can
ever maintain, a merely disinterested attitude
towards the trade or other economic relations
of its nationals with foreigners.   Governments admittedly are concerned with the
industry and commerce, foreign as well as
domestic, of their respective peoples, obtaining for that industry and commerce such

conditions as may secure for private effort and enterprise the best results. In this capacity they have always been accustomed to use the diplomatic machinery to secure for their " national " trade such liberties and opportunities in foreign lands as are attainable by arrangement with foreign Governments. Most of these arrangements consist in the removal or abatement of legal, fiscal, or other " artificial " restrictions, or in promoting the general safety of life and prosperity of their nationals. This work, done by diplomatic intercourse, special treaty stipulations, consular representations, etc., is work done by the State for the interest of the public as a whole. It is designed to strengthen and improve the commercial and other relations between the countries in question. But since this business is, in fact, conducted by certain firms or persons, whose interests are particularly engaged in it, the benefits of this State action are directly and chiefly reaped by them, and come home in enlarged private gains. But no one can advocate the total abstention of Governments from this work, on the ground that its direct gains are not equally distributed throughout the nation, but are of more advantage to certain individuals and classes than to others. The general effect of this consular and other Governmental action is to secure larger and freer opportunities for trade and investment for all members of the nation capable of engaging in such business, and some of the value of these enlarged business opportunities comes home to the nation as a whole in its capacity of a " consuming public."

It is doubtless a more controversial issue how far it is legitimate for a Government to employ political pressure to assist or advance the particular claims or interests of a firm or syndicate pushing a special financial deal, or contract, or concession, upon the Government or people of a foreign country, or to confer the semi-official authority of a charter upon a company claiming a monopoly of trade or developmental activities in some "backward area." But these practices have been so deep-set in the grooves of history that it is impossible to expect from any State a simple policy of renunciation. Business men have always looked to their Governments to secure for them fair or, if possible, preferential opportunities in business with foreign countries, and they have never looked in vain. Upon the whole, it would be urged, this policy of pushful business, aided by political support, has made for enlarged and freer commercial intercourse, and has been essential in the work of developing distant markets and more remote resources. It is inconceivable that Great Britain or any other civilized nation would be willing to renounce such political aids while other nations still retained them. Is it more conceivable that all Governments by simultaneous agreement should stand aside, giving no more support to their nationals in foreign trade or investments? Yet nothing can be more certain than that this competing support of Governments to foreign business enterprises of their countrymen must, if it continues, ripen new dangerous diplomatic situations, and form the substance of conflicting foreign policies and competing armaments. No League of Nations, no Hague Conventions, or other machinery for settling international disputes, are likely to furnish any reasonable security for peace or for reduced armaments, unless this problem of conflicting interests in the profitable exploitation of new markets and backward countries can be solved. Now there is only one line along which solution is possible. We cannot revert to strictly private enterprise, Governments looking on with folded arms, while private companies, with armed forces of their own, fasten political and economical dominion upon rubber or oil or gold fields in Africa or South America, enslaving or killing off the native population, as in San Thomé or Putumayo, and using up the rich natural resources of the country in a brief era of reckless waste. The only alternative is to advance to a settled policy of international arrangement for securing, if possible, that this commercial and developmental work shall in the future be conducted on a basis of pacific co-operation between the business groups in the respective countries under the joint control of their Governments.

This process of economic penetration and expansion cannot stop.   As more nations advance farther along the road of capitalist industry, the overflows of trade and capital, seeking more distant and more various fields of enterprise, will be stronger in their pressure.   This pressure has been the driving force in the modern Imperialism of the Western nations, stimulating them to discover " spheres of legitimate aspiration," " spheres of influence," " protectorates," " colonies," " places in the sun," and forcing their Governments into dangerous situations.   The process cannot stop.   But it may be possible to extract from it the poisonous sting of international rivalry. Why should not these necessary economic processes of expansion and development be carried on by pacific international arrange-

ments ? The germs of such arrangements
are to be found in the Congo Conference of
Berlin in 1884-85, in which were represented England, Germany, Austro-Hungary,
Belgium, Denmark, Spain, the United
States, France, Italy, Holland, Portugal,
Russia, Sweden-Norway, Turkey. "This
Conference stipulated freedom of commerce,
interdiction of slave-trade, and neutraliza-
tion of the territories in the Congo district,
and secured freedom of navigation on the
Rivers Congo and Niger."* A somewhat
similar international agreement was made,
first in 1880 at the Madrid Convention,
afterwards in 1906 at the Algeçiras Convention for the economic internationalization
of Morocco. Though in the earlier Convention only the nations immediately interested
were represented, the most notable outcome
was the extension to all nations of " the
most-favoured nation treatment," hitherto
confined to France and Britain. The treaty
was signed by all the Western European

* Oppenheim, " International Law," vol. ii., p. 71.

Powers and by the United States. Far more explicit, however, were the provisions for equality of economic opportunity furnished by the Act of Algeçiras. It provided not only for equality of trade, but for strict impartiality in loans and investments obtained from foreign countries. Still more important, the advantage of international over purely national control is shown in the provisions made for protecting the legitimate rights of the backward country which is the object of economic penetration.

As to the public services and the construction of public works, the Act declared that in no case should the rights of the " State over the public services of the Sheereefian Empire be alienated for the benefit of private interests." If the Moorish Government had recourse to foreign capital or industries in connection with the public services or public works, the Powers undertook to see that " the control of the State over such large undertakings of public interest remain intact "; tenders, " without respect of nationality," should regulate all orders for public works or the furnishing of supplies; no specification for orders should contain either "explicitly or implicitly any condition or provision of a nature to violate the principle of free competition or to place the competitors of one nationality at a disadvantage as against the competitors of another"; "regulations as to contracts should be drawn up by the Moorish Government and the Diplomatic Body at Tangier."*

This Agreement presents an excellent model for the larger policy of the Open Door, in defining the economic relations of the Governments and peoples of advanced towards backward countries. If all backward countries, whether under the political control of some European or other "advanced" State or still politically independent, were formally recognized by Conventions of the civilized Powers as similarly open to

* "Ten Years of Secret Diplomacy," by E. D. Morel, p. 31.

the trading and investing members of all countries on a basis of economic equality, with adequate mutual guarantees for the enforcement of the treaty obligations, the greatest step towards lasting and universal peace would have been taken.

It would need, however, to be supplemented and supported by other steps in order to achieve the full policy of equality of economic opportunity and to safeguard the interests of the inhabitants of backward areas thus brought within the area of economic internationalism. The substance of the Open Door policy may be stated in the following four proposals, which, in order to be effective, should be incorporated in a general Treaty or Convention signed by all the Powers:

1. Freedom of access for traders and goods of all nations to trade routes by land, river, canal, or sea, including the use of rail terminals, ports and coaling-stations, police protection and other facilities, upon terms of equality. Countries like Servia or Poland must not be at the mercy of possibly hostile

neighbours for commercial access to the out-side world. The export of wheat from Russia and Roumania must not be impeded in the future, as often in the past, by the closing of the Dardanelles. No Power must hold the keys of the Mediterranean or the Pacific. The Panama and Kiel Canals must be placed on the same basis of free use as the Suez Canal. No Power must reserve the right to close trade-gates at any time to traders of other nations.

2. Equal admission to markets and other trading facilities to be accorded by all Powers to foreign traders in all their dependencies.

This provision (an extension of the existing British practice) would leave it open to the Powers to retain tariff and other protection for their home markets. It would simply preclude them from extending the area of Protection to colonies, protectorates, and spheres of influence. Self-governing colonies, already possessing and exercising full control over their commercial and fiscal policy, would also be excluded from this stipulation.

3. Equal opportunities for the investment of capital in every form of business enter-prise and for full legal protection of all property for members of all nations in the dependencies of other nations.

4. The establishment of International

Commissions to secure equality of treatment for the commerce, investments and other property interests, of the subjects of the treaty Powers, in all backward or undeveloped countries not under the political control of any Power. Such Commissions might by concerted action exercise a restrictive control over the nature of the trade with "lower races," precluding, for example, the importation of arms or alcoholic liquors. They might also exercise a supervising authority over the loans and investments made by financiers to the Governments or private persons in these backward countries, and over the methods of business exploitation employed by the agents of the investing companies.

Whether these Commissions should endeavour to interpret "equality of opportunity" by some process of apportioning special spheres of interest and enterprise to the members of the several Powers, or whether they should encourage direct co-operation in the work of investment and development between business men of different nations, is a question into which I need not enter here. But readers may be reminded that control by International Commission is no untried method of regulating the diverse and conflicting interests of States. Four International Commissions have been instituted for dealing with questions of navigation, on the Danube, the Congo, and the Suez Canal. Three International Commissions have concerned themselves with questions of sanitation on the Lower Danube, at Constantinople, and at Alexandria. Three others are concerned with the interest of foreign creditors in Turkey, Egypt, and Greece, while a permanent Commission relating to sugar bounties was set up in 1902 by the Brussels Convention.

Why should not some such machinery by Commission be extended and endowed with adequate administrative powers, so as to form the nucleus of an efficient international Government regulating those economic relations between the advanced and backward peoples which are the most dangerous causes of dispute between modern Governments?

Taken in conjunction with the other applications of the Open Door, this direct endeavour to give a positive construction to the principle of equality of opportunity would seem to be the most feasible and efficacious way of dealing with the gravest practical problem of our time.*

This policy I present as the true alternative to the reactionary policy of economic nationalism urged by our New Protectionists in the name of defence. The true defence, the only possible security against future wars, is to extend and strengthen the bonds of economic and human intercourse between members of all nations, to remove the causes of economic antagonism which have hitherto bred dissension, and to substitute conditions of fair competition and fruitful co-operation. The issue is indeed a grave one. Are we to aim at breaking up the economic world into self-contained

* A vigorous and well-informed advocacy of International Commissions is contained in Mr. Lippmann's "The Stakes of Diplomacy" (Henry Holt and Co.).

nations, or groups of nations, not indifferent but actively hostile to one another in all parts of the earth, and incessantly engaged in fighting one another by tariffs, boycotts, Navigation Acts, and every weapon and barrier they can command, reducing the total productivity of the earth, increasing the difficulties of transport and commerce, and enforcing the application of an ever-growing proportion of each nation's wealth to war preparations which ever tend to fulfil the fearful purpose for which they are designed? Or are we to trust to the salutary effects of a Free Trade which has not yet been adequately tried, and to the extension of its principles to the new conditions of international intercourse by the establishment of public international control and guarantees? Place the risks and the difficulties of this latter policy as high as you choose, they fall immeasurably short of those to which the former policy exposes this nation and the world. The path of safety, as of opulence, lies in the forward

movement towards economic internationalism, not in a reversion towards a national
economy which for a country with our past
and present is impracticable, and, were it
practicable, would be none the less a be-
trayal of civilization for ourselves and for
humanity.

APPENDICES

APPENDIX A

RECOMMENDATIONS OF THE ECONOMIC CONFERENCE OF THE ALLIES HELD AT PARIS,

June 14, 15, 16, 17, 1916

I

THE representatives of the Allied Governments have met at Paris under the presidency of M. Clémentel, Minister of Commerce, on June 14, 15, 16, and 17, 1916, for the purpose of fulfilling the mandate given to them by the Paris Conference of March 28, 1916, of giving practical expression to their solidarity of views and interests, and of proposing to their respective Governments the appropriate measures for realizing this solidarity.

II

They declare that after forcing upon them the military contest, in spite of all their

141

efforts to avoid the conflict, the Empires of Central Europe are to-day preparing, in concert with their allies, for a contest on the economic plane, which will not only survive the re-establishment of peace, but will at that moment attain its full scope and intensity.

III

They cannot therefore conceal from themselves that the agreements which are being prepared for this purpose between their enemies have the obvious object of establishing the domination of the latter over the production and the markets of the whole world, and of imposing on other countries an intolerable yoke.

In face of so grave a peril, the representatives of the Allied Governments consider that it has become their duty, on grounds of necessary and legitimate defence, to adopt and realize from now onward all the measures requisite, on the one hand, to secure for themselves and for the whole of the markets of neutral countries full economic independence and respect for sound commercial practice ; and, on the other hand, to facilitate the organization on a permanent basis of their economic alliance.

For this purpose the representatives of the Allied Governments have decided to submit for the approval of those Governments the following resolutions :

A

MEASURES FOR THE WAR PERIOD

I

The laws and regulations prohibiting trading with the enemy shall be brought into accord.

For this purpose—

A.—The Allies will prohibit their own subjects and citizens and all persons residing in their territories from carrying on any trade with—

1. The inhabitants of enemy countries whatever their nationality.
2. Enemy subjects wherever resident.

3. Persons, firms, and companies, whose business is controlled wholly or partially by enemy subjects, or is subject to enemy influence and whose names are included in a special list.

B.—They will prohibit the importation into their territories of all goods originating in or coming from enemy countries.

C.—They will devise means of establishing a system enabling contracts entered into with enemy subjects and injurious to national interests to be cancelled unconditionally.

II

Business undertakings owned or operated by enemy subjects in the territories of the Allies will all be sequestrated or placed under control; measures will be taken for the purpose of winding up some of these undertakings and of realizing their assets, the proceeds of such realization remaining sequestrated or under control.

III

In addition to the export prohibitions which are necessitated by the internal situation of each of the Allied countries, the Allies will complete the measures already taken for the restriction of enemy supplies, both in the mother-countries and in the Dominions, Colonies, and Protectorates—

1. By unifying the lists of contraband and of export prohibition, and particularly by prohibiting the export of all commodities declared absolute or conditional contraband ;

2. By making the grant of licences for export to neutral countries from which export to enemy territories might take place conditional upon the existence in such countries of control organiza-

10

tions approved by the Allies; or,
in the absence of such organiza-
tions, upon special guarantees
such as the limitation of the
quantities exported, supervision
by Allied consular officers, etc.

B

TRANSITORY MEASURES FOR THE PERIOD OF COMMERCIAL, INDUSTRIAL, AGRICULTURAL, AND MARITIME RECONSTRUCTION OF THE ALLIED COUNTRIES

I

The Allies declare their common determi-
nation to insure the re-establishment of the
countries suffering from acts of destruction,
spoliation and unjust requisition, and decide
to join in devising means to secure the
restoration to those countries, as a prior
claim, of their raw materials, industrial and
agricultural plant, stock and mercantile fleet,
or to assist them to re-equip themselves in
these respects.

II

Whereas the war has put an end to all the treaties of commerce between the Allies and the Enemy Powers, and whereas it is of essential importance that, during the period of economic reconstruction which will follow the cessation of hostilities, the liberty of none of the Allies should be hampered by any claim put forward by the Enemy Powers to most-favoured-nation treatment, the Allies agree that the benefit of this treatment shall not be granted to those Powers during a number of years to be fixed by mutual agreement among themselves.

During this number of years the Allies undertake to assure to each other so far as possible compensatory outlets for trade in case consequences detrimental to their commerce result from the application of the undertaking referred to in the preceding paragraph.

III

The Allies declare themselves agreed to conserve for the Allied countries, before all others, their natural resources during the whole period of commercial, industrial, agricultural, and maritime reconstruction, and for this purpose they undertake to establish special arrangements to facilitate the interchange of these resources.

IV

In order to defend their commerce, their industry, their agriculture, and their navigation, against economic aggression resulting from dumping or any other mode of unfair competition, the Allies decide to fix by agreement a period of time during which the commerce of the Enemy Powers shall be submitted to special treatment, and the goods originating in their countries shall be subjected either to prohibitions or to a special régime of an effective character.

The Allies will determine by agreement through diplomatic channels the special conditions to be imposed during the above-mentioned period on the ships of the Enemy Powers.

V

The Allies will devise the measures to be taken jointly or severally for preventing enemy subjects from exercising, in their territories, certain industries or professions which concern national defence or economic independence.

C

PERMANENT MEASURES OF MUTUAL ASSISTANCE AND COLLABORATION AMONG THE ALLIES

I

The Allies decide to take the necessary steps without delay to render themselves independent of the enemy countries in so far as regards the raw materials and manufactured articles essential to the normal development of their economic activities.

These steps should be directed to assuring the independence of the Allies not only so far as concerns their sources of supply, but also as regards their financial, commercial, and maritime organization.

The Allies will adopt the methods which seem to them most suitable for the carrying out of this resolution, according to the nature of the commodities and having regard to the principles which govern their economic policy.

They may, for example, have recourse either to enterprises subsidized, directed, or controlled, by the Governments themselves, or to the grant of financial assistance for the encouragement of scientific and technical research and the development of national industries and resources; to Customs duties or prohibitions of a temporary or permanent character; or to a combination of these different methods.

Whatever may be the methods adopted, the object aimed at by the Allies is to increase production within their territories as a whole to a sufficient extent to enable them to maintain and develop their economic position and independence in relation to enemy countries.

II

In order to permit the interchange of their products, the Allies undertake to adopt measures for facilitating their mutual trade relations both by the establishment of direct and rapid land and sea transport services at low rates, and by the extension and improvement of postal, telegraphic, and other communications.

III

The Allies undertake to convene a meeting of technical delegates to draw up measures for the assimilation, so far as may be possible, of their laws governing patents, indications of origin, and trade-marks.

In regard to patents, trade-marks, and literary and artistic copyright, which have come into existence during the war in enemy countries, the Allies will adopt, so far as possible, an identical procedure, to be applied as soon as hostilities cease.

This procedure will be elaborated by the technical delegates of the Allies.

D

Whereas for the purposes of their common defence against the enemy the Allied Powers have agreed to adopt a common economic policy, on the lines laid down in the Resolutions which have been passed, and whereas it is recognized that the effectiveness of this policy depends absolutely upon these Resolutions being put into operation forthwith, the representatives of the Allied Governments undertake to recommend their respective Governments to take without delay all the measures, whether temporary or permanent, requisite for giving full and complete effect to this policy forthwith, and to communicate to each other the decisions arrived at to attain that object.

Board of Trade,
June 21, 1916.

www.ingramcontent.com/pod-product-compliance
Lightning Source LLC
Chambersburg PA
CBHW020545270326
41927CB00006B/727